Sweet Confections

Sweet Confections

BEAUTIFUL CANDY TO MAKE AT HOME

Nina Wanat

LARK

An Imprint of Sterling Publishing Co., Inc.
New York

WWW.LARKCRAFTS.COM

EDITOR: Beth Sweet

ART DIRECTOR: Kristi Pfeffer

PHOTOGRAPHERS: Diane Cu and Todd Porter

COVER DESIGNER: Amy Sly

Library of Congress Cataloging-in-Publication Data

Wanat, Nina.
  Sweet confections : beautiful candy to make at home / Nina Wanat. -- 1st ed.
      p. cm.
  Includes index.
  ISBN 978-1-60059-920-0 (pb-trade pbk. : alk. paper)
  1. Candy. I. Title.
  TX791.W25 2011
  641.8'53--dc22

                                                    2011001867

10 9 8 7 6 5 4 3 2 1

First Edition

Published by Lark Crafts
An Imprint of Sterling Publishing Co., Inc.
387 Park Avenue South, New York, NY 10016

Text © 2011, Nina Wanat
Photography © 2011, Lark Crafts, an Imprint of Sterling Publishing Co., Inc.,
unless otherwise specified

Distributed in Canada by Sterling Publishing,
c/o Canadian Manda Group, 165 Dufferin Street
Toronto, Ontario, Canada M6K 3H6

Distributed in the United Kingdom by GMC Distribution Services,
Castle Place, 166 High Street, Lewes, East Sussex, England BN7 1XU

Distributed in Australia by Capricorn Link (Australia) Pty Ltd.,
P.O. Box 704, Windsor, NSW 2756 Australia

If you have questions or comments about this book, please contact:

Lark Crafts
67 Broadway
Asheville, NC 28801
828-253-0467

Manufactured in China

ISBN 13: 978-1-60059-920-0

For information about custom editions, special sales, premium and corporate
purchases, please contact Sterling Special Sales Department at 800-805-5489 or
specialsales@sterlingpub.com.

For information about desk and examination copies available to college and university
professors, requests must be submitted to academic@larkbooks.com. Our complete
policy can be found at www.larkcrafts.com.

✳ Contents

Crunchy Candy

Chewy Candy

Silky Candy

128 In the Pantry

Introduction

aking candy does not simply make you feel like a kid in a candy store—it makes you feel like a kid with *keys* to the candy store. You get to enjoy everything about the sweet and unique process, from selecting your favorite flavors, to overseeing the cooking, to sharing your creations with delighted family and friends.

There are tales of wily candymakers throughout the ages who kept the secrets of their trade to themselves in order to preserve their mystique and singularity, but I think one of the best-kept secrets is that the candymaking process itself is quite a treat. If you've never made candy before, you will be amazed by the transformation of familiar ingredients—such as sugar, butter, and milk—into awe-inspiring confections. There is nothing better than watching an unassumingly transparent sugar syrup whip up into a pristine white billow of marshmallow fluff or witnessing a freshly dipped truffle gradually acquire a firm and glossy shell after being submerged in melted chocolate. If you've previously boiled pots and pots of peanut brittle or devised your own clever version of a nutty chocolate bark, then you are already privy to the magic of the process. And you don't need a fancy commercial kitchen or grandiose appliances to transform your ideas into luscious Pumpkin Caramels (page 70) or decadent Coconut Shells (page 124). This book (and a few basic tools) will have you ready to whip up a batch of deliciousness in no time.

Beautiful candymaking is easy and within your reach, and I'm here to guide you through it. No matter how exotic the recipe may seem, candymaking can usually be summed up as either a way of boiling and cooling sugar or a way of melting and shaping chocolate. While I am humbly proud of these recipes, I am also a fervent believer that any fresh candy made with care and good ingredients cannot be beat, period. Read through the Getting Started section that follows to acquaint (or perhaps re-acquaint!) yourself with the main ingredients, tools, and techniques used to make candy. Then follow any of the recipes in this book, and you'll be rewarded with candy that tastes and looks better than anything you can buy.

Beautiful candy often inspires nostalgic reveries of a holiday or loved one, and the classic, traditional taste of sweets like Toffee (page 38) and Vanilla Marshmallows (page 116) can elicit trips down memory lane. At the same time, candymaking is also an exciting way to experiment with new flavors and forms. It's the addition (or sometimes substitution) of an unexpected ingredient that keeps the craft contemporary and exciting. Why not top toffee with smoked almonds instead of roasted almonds? Are you guilty of nibbling away at the dough while baking cookies? Hold the shame, and instead try Chocolate Chip Cookie Dough Fudge (page 100). You know that peanut butter goes well with jelly, but have you ever tasted it with maple syrup in an

"If you've never made candy before, you will be amazed by the transformation of familiar ingredients—such as sugar, butter, and milk—into awe-inspiring confections."

oat-laced Peanut Butter & Maple Praline (page 114)? Timeless tastes, intense flavors, and riveting textures—whether they're crunchy, chewy, or silky—are the stuff of candy legends.

There is no better way to treat the tastebuds in your community than to share the sweet rewards of your craft. If you're making a variety of candies for gifts, part of the fun is thinking about how each confection can stand alone to be admired while at the same time pleasantly complementing all of the others. If, on the other hand, you want to satisfy a single craving, a stylish box filled with uniform pieces of show-stopping candy is more than a gift—it's a display of skill, care, and love.

I hope that this book inspires and delights your candymaking sensibilities. It is often said that confectionery is based on science and precision, but it is surprisingly flexible to your tastes. I'm confident that some of these recipes will become your family favorites, and it won't be long before you know automatically when to infuse or include your favorite flavors, and when to boil a few degrees higher or lower to suit your preference for texture. Your kitchen and your imagination await—let your creativity and sweet tooth guide you on the satisfying path of crafting beautiful candy.

Getting Started
Making Sweet Confections

Have you ever noticed how candy stores, with their gleaming displays of treasures, resemble jewelry stores? Candy is the most gem-like of foods—vibrantly colored, exquisitely shaped, dazzling with sparkle or alluring with rich texture.

Making your own candy may seem exotic or complicated, but, as you'll see once you explore the recipes in this book, most candymaking is essentially a matter of boiling and cooling sugar or melting and shaping chocolate. You don't need to be concerned with perfection—it's candy, have fun!—but because there is some science to the art of candymaking, you do need to pay a little more attention to details than usual. If you're new to candymaking, familiarize yourself now with the ingredients, tools, and techniques I call for in the recipes that follow.

From Top:
Maple syrup,
white sugar,
honey, brown
sugar, corn
syrup, and
molasses;
White, milk, and
dark chocolate;
Whipping cream,
real unsalted
butter, and
whole milk

Ingredients for Candymaking

A wide variety of ingredients can be used to make candy, so be sure to use those that taste the best to you.

SWEETENERS

Granulated sugar is the main building block of candy. Its neutral flavor and familiar sweetness make it an ideal base for flavors to shine through. Caramelized, its flavor becomes more complex and assertive.

Brown sugar has molasses added back to it after the refining process. It can't be caramelized because of its impurities, but, in traditional recipes, brown sugar is often used to impart a caramel-like flavor to candy.

Corn syrup is a liquid sugar that imparts sweetness while acting as what's called a "doctor" to prevent crystallization of the granulated sugar in the candy.

Maple syrup can add wonderful flavor and sweetness to candy. I recommend using "Grade B" maple syrup, which has a more intense flavor than "Grade A."

Molasses is a by-product of the sugar refining process. The recipes in this book were tested with unsulphured light molasses.

Honey is another source of flavor and sweetness for candy. I like the neutrally floral flavor of wildflower honey, but if you have your own favorite variety, feel free to try it.

CHOCOLATES

There are so many exciting chocolates available these days. In general, I recommend using blended, neutral-tasting chocolates for candymaking, so the chocolate won't overpower or conflict with the filling, but don't be afraid to experiment with whatever you enjoy eating. Callebaut, Valrhona, Scharffenberger, Ghirardelli, and Guittard make good quality chocolate that can be purchased in slab form for candymaking.

Chocolate is usually made of cocoa solids (cocoa powder and cocoa butter), sugar, vanilla, and lecithin. Cocoa butter is one of the few vegetable fats that is solid at room temperature, so it can also be used as a firming agent in candy recipes such as nougat.

For dark chocolate, I recommend using bittersweet chocolate with 55 to 65 percent cocoa solids. Milk chocolate should contain about 30 percent cocoa solids. White chocolate does not contain the cocoa powder part of cocoa solids, but it is required to contain at least 20 percent cocoa butter.

Chocolate that's melted for recipes needs to be tempered (see How to Temper Chocolate, page 20). Coating chocolate (also called compound or dipping chocolate) is a convenient option that doesn't contain cocoa butter, so it doesn't need to be tempered. Once melted, coating chocolate is ready to be dipped or molded. It can be found online, at large craft stores, and in the produce section of some grocery stores (since it's used to dip fruits).

DAIRY

Due to its fat content, dairy adds flavor, richness, and a distinct texture to candy. It's important to use real unsalted butter, whipping cream, and whole milk for the recipes in this book for the proper results. Margarine and low-fat substitutes just won't work in the same ways.

BUTTER & OIL

Butter doesn't need to be at room temperature when used in boiled candy, such as toffee, but for recipes where it will be mixed in uncooked, such as the Pastel Butter Mints (page 126), it should be softened to room temperature before use.

A neutral oil, such as a canola or vegetable oil, should be used as non-stick agents in pans. Spray oils work well, or you could dab oil on a paper towel to spread in the pan.

Clockwise from top left:
Eggs and cream of tartar;
Rum, bourbon, pear liqueur, and tequila;
Hazelnuts, pecans, cashews, walnuts, almonds,
peanuts, pistachios, coconut, and macadamias

EGGS

Use large eggs for the recipes in this book, and keep them refrigerated. They don't need to be brought to room temperature when making candy.

SPICES & SALT

Heat helps to release the flavor of spices, so it's best to make spiced candy with ground spices that are added at the beginning of cooking. Cinnamon and allspice are especially popular around the winter holidays for their festive, warming flavors that go well with fruits and nuts, while cayenne is especially refreshing during the hotter months. At the base of many delicious candy recipes is the sweet, light flavor of vanilla: learn to create your own vanilla extract in the book's Pantry section (page 130).

Cream of Tartar: This acidic ingredient helps prevent crystallization in candy.

Salt: The recipes in this book were tested with kosher salt. Large-crystal finishing salts are excellent garnishes to enhance the flavors of your candy. Flaky sea salt, mineral-tinged fleur de sel, earthy pink salt, and pungent smoked salt are all good options.

NUTS

Peanuts, almonds, pistachios, pecans, walnuts, coconut, cashews, macadamias, and hazelnuts are used in this book. Different types of nuts can be used interchangeably in any of these recipes, depending on your taste preference, and you may also try pine nuts or Brazil nuts. Roasting the nuts is optional, but many people, including me, find that roasting enriches their flavor and makes them crisper. Nuts are best chopped with a chef's knife because a food processor will not cut them evenly. Store nuts in the refrigerator or freezer to keep them tasting fresh longer, and taste them before use to make sure they're not rancid.

ALCOHOL

Bourbon, tequila, pear liqueur, and rum are used in this book, and I recommended that you use quality liquor. Only use alcohol that you enjoy the taste of in your candy. Hard liquors can be substituted for one another in recipes if you'd like to create your own flavor profiles, but, in general, try to use young, potent liquor whose flavor will be strong enough to come through the other ingredients.

Tools

Baking Pans. These pans have high sides, and when lined with parchment paper, can be used to pour candy into to set. The recipes in this book call for 8 x 8-inch baking pans.

Baking Sheet Liners. Parchment paper and non-stick silicone mats are invaluable as non-stick surfaces for candies. They're interchangeable except that parchment paper can be folded to fit baking pans.

Baking Sheets. These usually measure 12 x 18 inches, and their flat surface and low sides are perfect to use for dipped candies. Don't use warped baking sheets, or your candy will also turn out warped.

Bowls. I prefer stainless steel bowls for mixing ingredients and to use as the tops of double boilers. They're light-weight, odor-resistant, and sturdy. Glass bowls can be used to melt chocolate in the microwave.

Dipping Forks. Chocolate-dipping forks are available with two or three tines; many find that the three tines offer greater stability. I like to bend the tines up about 45° so that the fork forms a reclined L shape for ease of dipping and holding. If an uneven puddle of chocolate forms under your dipped candy, the culprit could be the fork—make sure that the tines are perfectly aligned.

Double Boiler. Although you can buy a double boiler pot set, I find that a stainless steel bowl set over a saucepan of water is the best option because it's the easiest set-up for stirring ingredients.

Food-Safe Gloves. Only use gloves that are marked as "food-safe" to handle the candy as you're cooking (I purchase mine from drug stores.) As you wear them, wash them and dry them with paper towels as you would your hands. They will keep your hands clean and your candy sanitary.

Knives. A serrated knife, with large teeth along its edge, is the best option for chopping chocolate. Otherwise, a chef's knife, with a straight edge, can be used to chop nuts, fruit, and marshmallows.

Molds. Chocolate will take on the complexion of a surface it touches; glossy molds let you form chocolate into interesting shapes with an attractive glossy surface. Chocolate molds are either lightweight plastic or heavy-duty polycarbonate. Hard candy molds are made from silicone, tempered plastic, or metal in order to withstand heat.

Pastry Brushes. I prefer silicone brushes to bristle brushes because they don't "shed" into the candy.

Pizza Wheel. This implement is perfect for cutting slabs of candy quickly.

Ruler or Straightedge. A clean kitchen ruler or straightedge with measurements comes in handy for cutting candy into straight lines.

Saucepans. Heavyweight stainless steel saucepans are the best for even heat conduction.

Spatulas. Heatproof silicone spatulas are preferred for stirring boiled sugar syrups. They are also perfect for stirring chocolate because they allow you to cleanly scrape the sides of the bowl with their flat but flexible edges. Offset metal spatulas, which have a bend in their oblong stainless steel blades, are preferred for smoothing the tops of warm slabs of candy.

Stand Mixer. A sturdy 5-quart stand mixer is required to make marshmallows and nougat. Unfortunately, hand mixers and elbow grease lack the power and speed to aerate sugar properly.

Thermometers. These are crucial for making chocolate and candy. A chocolate thermometer must give readings between 80°F and 120°F, and either a glass, non-mercury thermometer or a digital, infrared surface thermometer will work well.

For candymaking, the thermometer must give readings between 220°F and 310°F. A clip-on candy thermometer should be read at eye level for accurate readings. Its calibration can be checked by immersing it in boiling water to ensure that it reads 212°F. If the reading is off, get a new one, and keep that adjustment in mind if cooking in the meantime. You can also use digital instant-read thermometers with probes. Never allow the thermometer to touch the bottom of a saucepan while cooking or else the reading will be inaccurate.

Wooden Spoons. These are best to stir hot candies that are thick and need to be coated, such as Sour Cream Candied Nuts (page 58). They're more rugged than silicone spatulas (and just as heat-resistant), but they don't scrape the bottoms and sides of pots as thoroughly during cooking and so are not preferred for all recipes.

From top left: Baking pans and baking sheets; Parchment paper, silicone mats, and candy molds; Stainless steel bowls and glass bowls; Offset metal spatula, silicone spatula, wooden spoon, candy thermometer, chocolate thermometer, pastry brush, knife, dipping forks, and pizza cutter

Below: Chef's knife (left); Serrated knife (right)

Candymaking Techniques

HOW TO TEMPER CHOCOLATE

If you simply melt chocolate, the fat molecules in the cocoa butter will separate, and it will set with unattractive white streaks and a soft, uneven texture. Tempering is a method of heating and cooling chocolate so that the fat crystals re-form and give the chocolate an attractive hard, glossy finish.

The "seeding method" is a quick and easy way to temper chocolate. It is essentially adding reserved pieces of the chopped chocolate (called the seed) into the melting chocolate. As this unmelted chocolate releases its "good" crystals into the melted chocolate, the fat molecules in the melted chocolate reform into the desired configuration, and you have the perfect melted chocolate to make attractive candies.

Plan to temper at least one pound of chocolate at a time so that you can maintain its temperature with ease. Temper chocolate right before you're going to use it; otherwise, the good crystals will continue to multiply over time, and the chocolate will become too thick and set with a dull, speckled finish. Tempering should be done in a room that's between 65°F and 70°F. If it's much cooler or warmer, the chocolate will either set too slowly or too quickly. You'll need a chocolate thermometer to make sure your melting temperatures are exactly right.

Steps to Temper Chocolate

Chop the chocolate. Use a serrated knife on a sturdy cutting board to cut the chocolate into pieces no larger than ½ inch per side Ⓐ to ensure that the chocolate will melt evenly over low heat. The best way to chop a slab of chocolate with minimal effort is to start chopping diagonally at one corner and shift the slab so that your knife can take on new corners as they form.

Melt two-thirds of the chocolate, reserving one-third as seed chocolate Ⓑ. Dark chocolate should be fully melted to 115°F, and milk and white chocolates to 112°F. To use a double boiler, heat the chocolate in a stainless steel bowl set atop a saucepan of barely simmering water. Stir occasionally with a silicone spatula Ⓒ so that the chocolate melts evenly. When fully melted, remove the chocolate from the heat, but let the water continue to simmer so that it can be used to reheat the chocolate later. Be sure to dry the bottom of the bowl with a towel so that water doesn't drip onto your workspace.

To use a microwave, heat the chocolate in a microwave-safe bowl for 30 seconds. Stir, and repeat until half of the chocolate is melted and the bowl feels warm. Adjust the microwave to 50 percent power, and heat in 5- to 10-second intervals until it's fully melted. Stir between each interval.

Seed the chocolate. Reserve one handful of the seed chocolate (the remaining one-third of chopped chocolate) and stir the rest into the bowl of melted chocolate . Let the chocolate cool down to 93°F, stirring occasionally. If all of this chocolate seed melts, add in the reserved handful of seed chocolate and let it melt.

Let the chocolate cool down slightly: Stir dark chocolate until it reaches 88°F. Stir milk or white chocolate until it reaches 86°F. The seed should now be completely melted, but if any remains, remove it.

Reheat the chocolate. Set the bowl atop the double boiler for 3-second intervals (or heat in the microwave for 3-second intervals at 50 percent power), stirring and checking the temperature, between each interval. Bring the chocolate to its ideal working temperature for dipping or coating (dark chocolate to 90°F and milk and white chocolates to 88°F).

Test the chocolate. Dip a piece of parchment paper or a spoon into the chocolate, and set it on the work surface. If the chocolate sets shiny and smooth within 3 to 5 minutes, congratulations! Your chocolate is in good temper and is ready to be used. If it's streaky, try stirring in more chopped chocolate, and testing again in 5 minutes.

Above: Dip a piece of parchment paper into the chocolate to test its temper. The test on the left is streaky and not yet tempered. The test on the right is shiny and smooth and correctly tempered.

Keep the chocolate tempered. Once the chocolate is tempered and at its ideal working temperature, you must use it before it cools and sets. If the chocolate falls four degrees below its ideal working temperature, you can gently reheat it, but don't let it exceed the ideal working temperature. Heat for 3-second intervals, stirring and checking the temperature between each. If the chocolate is in a stainless steel bowl, you can also warm it with a hair dryer or heat gun for 8-second intervals.

If you have leftover tempered chocolate, you can save it for future use by pouring the chocolate out onto parchment paper, letting it set, breaking it into pieces, and then storing it in an airtight container. You'll need to temper this chocolate again before using it in recipes calling for tempered chocolate.

GETTING STARTED

HOW TO DIP CANDIES IN CHOCOLATE

Candies dipped in chocolate look beautiful, taste delicious, and always impress. In order to achieve flawless results that showcase your hard work, take time to organize your workspace so that dipping can flow smoothly and you can maintain the ideal working temperature for your tempered chocolate. Starting from left to right, place the pan of candy centers to be dipped, the bowl of tempered chocolate, the bowl of coating ingredients (for hand-rolled candies), a parchment-lined baking sheet to hold the candies for setting, and any garnishes that will be sprinkled on top.

Hand-Rolling Round Candies

It's best to hand-roll round truffles or candies. Put on food-safe gloves, spoon tempered chocolate into the palm of one hand and add the candy center Ⓐ. Then roll the candy and chocolate between your two gloved hands until the candy center is completely covered with chocolate Ⓑ. Roll the covered candy off your hand and into the bowl of coating ingredients Ⓒ, such as cocoa powder or powdered sugar. Use a spoon to completely cover the candy. Continue until the bowl is full of truffles and their coatings have set. Remember to keep a close eye on the temperature of your chocolate to be sure it remains tempered and at ideal working temperature. Use a dipping fork to remove each candy onto the prepared baking sheet.

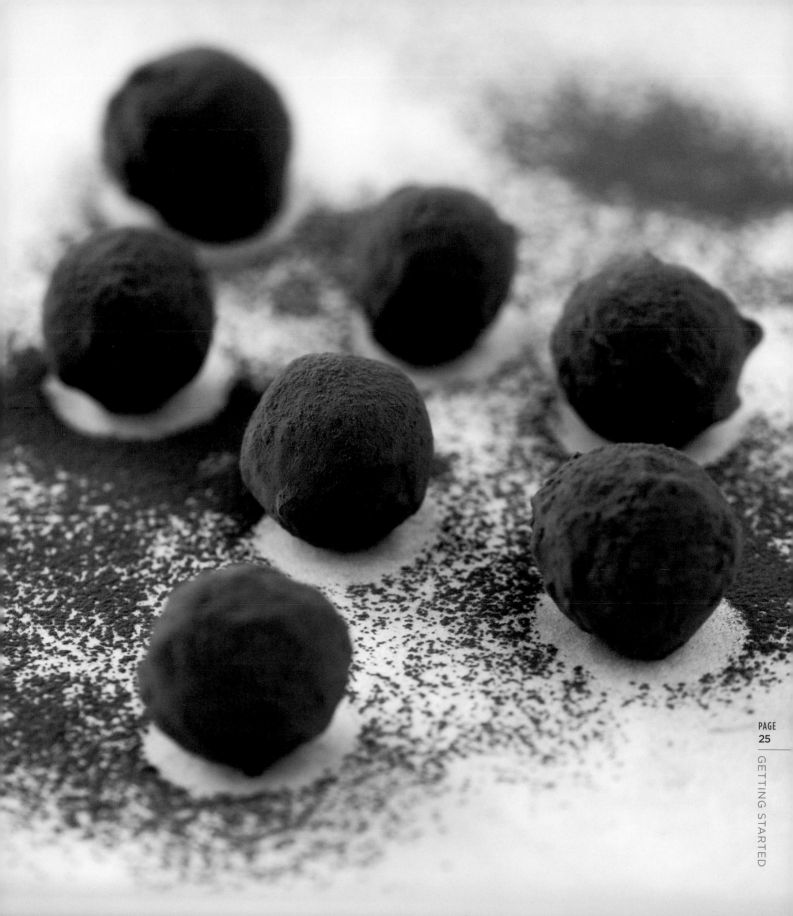

Dipping Rectangular Candies

For rectangular candies, it is best to use two dipping forks, with one in each gloved hand. Place the candy in the bowl of chocolate, and submerge it with a dipping fork (A). Slide the dipping fork just halfway underneath the candy, and lift it out of the chocolate (B). Move the candy up and down so that its bottom just touches the top surface of the chocolate. This will help remove excess chocolate from around the piece. Finish the job by scraping the bottom of the candy with the second dipping fork (C). Place the candy on the prepared baking sheet by setting down the edge that overhangs the fork first, then lowering the fork, and sliding it out from under the piece (D). Remember to keep a close eye on the temperature of your chocolate to be sure it remains tempered and at ideal working temperature.

E

It's a lot easier to add garnishes to dipped candy in batches instead of dipping and garnishing one at a time. To do so, start dipping your candy centers in the chocolate, and keep going until the first one looks slightly matted—now you'll need to stop and add the garnish. Clean your gloved hand of any chocolate residue with a paper towel, and sprinkle or place the garnish onto all of the pieces ⓔ. With a second paper towel, clear your dipping forks of any solidified chocolate before continuing to dip.

If your candy doesn't have a garnish, you can make decorative marks with a dipping fork instead. Wait until the dipped chocolate is just thickening, and press the tines of the dipping fork flat into the chocolate and then pull up and to one side ⓕ. You can use three- and two-tine forks to make different patterns that will look beautiful and help identify the flavor.

F

GETTING STARTED

HOW TO COOK SUGAR

Familiar and seemingly unassuming granulated white sugar is the primary structural ingredient of candy. It's also surprisingly versatile. Sugar can be used to make candies with an infinite variety of textures and flavors. Ending up with the texture and flavor you desire will depend mainly on two things: the temperatures at which you cook and cool the sugar and the procedures you use while cooking. Before you get started, you'll need a good candy thermometer, a clean bowl to hold the finished product, and some sugar syrup know-how.

From left: If you stir a boiling sugar syrup that *shouldn't* be stirred, you'll get a pan full of rock hard crystallized sugar. If you don't stir a boiling sugar syrup that *should* be stirred, the syrup will scorch.

To Stir, or Not to Stir

Most candies are made by boiling sugar and water into a sugar syrup that's cooked to different stages of firmness. The most important factor during the boiling is whether or not the syrup should be stirred. If you stir a boiling sugar syrup that shouldn't be stirred, the sugar crystals will cling to each other and multiply, leaving you with a saucepan of rock-hard crystallized sugar. On the other hand, if you don't stir a boiling sugar syrup that should be stirred, the syrup will scorch. The recipes in this book will let you know whether or not to stir.

In general, recipes that include butter, cream, or other dairy products need to be stirred while boiling so that the dairy solids cook evenly and don't scorch. The fat in the dairy prevents the sugar from crystallizing while being stirred, and the cooking develops the dairy's flavor. You're not stirring to emulsify or mix together ingredients, so it's best to always stir slowly and gently. Keep the spatula in continual contact with the bottom or sides of the saucepan so that the boiling sugar syrup will not splash out—and onto you! If you notice that one area of the saucepan is especially hot and boiling more than the rest of the pan, take care to stir that area frequently. Don't agitate dairy-based candies as they are cooling down, or the fat may separate out of the candy.

Typically, sugar syrups that don't include dairy (such as those for taffy and hard candies) should not be stirred as they are boiling. However, these sugar syrups do sometimes require agitation as they cool down in order to achieve a certain texture.

Above: Boiling sugar and water into a sugar syrup

How to Cook Sugar Syrup

This is the method to use when water is added to sugar so that it can be cooked to a certain stage of firmness (i.e., soft ball, hard crack). The stages of cooked sugar might seem intimidating at first, but just keep in mind that you're really just boiling the sugar syrup to remove a certain amount of moisture. The longer the syrup boils and the higher the temperature climbs, the more steam escapes the pan and leaves behind a drier and harder candy.

Begin by pouring water into the pan, and then add the sugar. (The amount of water and sugar added will vary according to the specific recipe you're using.)

Place the pan over the level of heat called for in the recipe, and stir gently until the sugar syrup comes to a rolling boil. Make sure that all of the sugar is dissolved. If crystals of sugar form on the side of the saucepan above the water line, dab them with a wet pastry brush until they are thoroughly dissolved.

After the sugar syrup has come to a boil, clip a candy thermometer on the side of the pan. Don't clip the thermometer on before the syrup boils because sugar crystals may collect around it and remain undissolved.

When the sugar syrup has come to the temperature called for in the recipe, immediately remove the pan from the heat, and pour out the syrup into a clean bowl. Don't scrape the final contents from the bottom of the pan—they're inevitably firmer than the syrup you poured out first.

Tips: *If the temperature of your syrup exceeds the prescribed temperature in the recipe, all is not lost. Simply add a couple tablespoons of water to the syrup. The temperature will fall, and you can proceed to take it to the correct temperature.*

The best and fastest way to remove cooked sugar from the inside of a pan is to fill it with water and bring it to a boil on the stovetop. Once the sugar dissolves, wash the pan thoroughly.

1. THREAD 230-234°F
Syrup forms a thin string.

2. SOFT BALL 235-240°F
Syrup holds its shape as a soft ball for a few seconds.

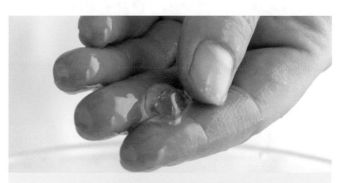

3. FIRM BALL 241-249°F
Syrup holds its shape as a ball, but is still malleable.

4. HARD BALL 250-269°F
Syrup forms a ball that cannot be flattened.

5. SOFT CRACK 270-290°F
Syrup holds its shape and bends a little before breaking.

6. HARD CRACK 295-310°F
Syrup is solid and breaks with pressure.

7. CARAMEL 320-350°F
Syrup is brown and brittle.

HOW TO CARAMELIZE SUGAR

This dry method of caramelization lets you take a bowl of granulated white sugar and turn it into a saucepan of deep brown liquid caramel without adding any other ingredients. This dry method cooks the sugar so quickly that it cannot be stopped at the various sugar stages, such as soft ball or hard crack. Once sugar is caramelized, it can be stirred without risk of crystallization because the crystals have already been broken down. It's often then used as an ingredient in candies, such as chewy caramels, that benefit from its complex dimensions of flavor.

Heat an empty saucepan on medium high for a few minutes.

Pour about a ⅛-inch layer of sugar into the saucepan. If necessary, shake the pan from side to side to get an even layer A.

Wherever you first notice a darkened spot of brown caramelized sugar, begin stirring in that spot with a silicone spatula. Gradually swirl the surrounding sugar into the liquefied caramel B. At this point, the caramel should still look like a thick tan syrup that's coarse with crystals.

Add another ⅛-inch layer of sugar C. Gradually stir it into the caramelized sugar, taking care not to add too much granulated sugar to the caramelized sugar at one time, or it will be too thick to stir. The sugar should stay mostly liquid.

Keep adding layers of sugar one at a time to the saucepan until it is all incorporated D.

Stir the sugar so that it cooks evenly until all of the sugar crystals are dissolved and the caramel is amber E. You can check for crystals by tilting the pan up and looking for any crystals in the thinnest part of the caramel. The caramel is now ready to be used in your recipe F.

GETTING STARTED

Safety Precautions

Boiled sugar syrups can be very hot—sometimes 100°F hotter than boiling water—and also very sticky. Always keep a bowl of ice water near you while cooking. If hot sugar splashes onto your hands, immediately plunge them into the water. Do not try to rub hot sugar off with your other hand—it will only stick and burn it, too.

Crunchy Candy

Toffee

MAKES ABOUT 1½ pounds

While toffee is a delicious expression of butter, sugar, and salt all on its own, it can be coated with chocolate on one or both sides and have mix-ins in the toffee as well as on the chocolate. You can get creative with graham crackers, cookies, nuts, dried fruit, salt, or most any other dry food in your cabinets.

METHOD

● Line a baking sheet with parchment paper.

● Boil the water, butter, cream, sugar, and salt over medium heat in a 3-quart saucepan. Stir slowly and constantly with a heatproof spatula until the syrup reaches 300°F.

● Remove the mixture from the heat, and stir in the vanilla, if using. Pour onto the parchment paper. Let stand 1 minute, then sprinkle chocolate on top of the toffee. Wait 3 to 5 minutes for the chocolate to melt, then spread it evenly over the toffee with an offset spatula. Sprinkle on the almonds, followed by the salt, if using.

● Refrigerate the toffee until the chocolate is set, about 45 minutes. Break into pieces, and store in an airtight container.

VARIATIONS:

Smoked Almond Toffee: Replace the roasted almonds with smoked almonds.

Pistachio & White Chocolate Toffee: Replace the toppings with roasted pistachios, pink Hawaiian salt, and white chocolate.

YOU WILL NEED

Baking sheet

Parchment paper

3-quart saucepan

Heatproof silicone spatula

Candy thermometer

Offset spatula

1 tablespoon water

2 sticks (1 cup) butter, cut into cubes

¼ cup cream

1 cup sugar

½ teaspoon salt

½ teaspoon vanilla extract (optional) (page 130)

5 ounces dark chocolate or coating chocolate, chopped

1 cup roasted almonds, chopped (page 134)

Flakey sea salt, for sprinkling (optional)

Peanut Brittle

MAKES ABOUT 1 pound

Roasted peanuts are the secret to this rich and resonant brittle. Raw peanuts will only toast on the outside during the cooking process, leaving much of their flavor untapped.

YOU WILL NEED

Baking sheet
Parchment paper
Pastry brush
Heatproof silicone spatula
Candy thermometer
Offset spatula

¼ cup water
1 cup sugar
½ cup corn syrup
1¼ cups roasted peanuts (page 134)
3 tablespoons butter
1½ teaspoons kosher salt
¾ teaspoon vanilla extract (page 130)
¾ teaspoon baking soda

METHOD

● Line a baking sheet with parchment paper.

● Mix together the water, sugar, and corn syrup in a 2-quart saucepan until all of the sugar is wet. If sugar crystals cling to the sides of the pan, dissolve them away with a wet pastry brush.

● Bring the mixture to a boil over medium-high heat, stirring occasionally and gently with a heatproof spatula until all of the sugar is dissolved. Then boil to 250°F without stirring.

● Add the peanuts and the butter, stirring constantly and gently until the mixture reaches 320°F.

● Remove from the heat, and stir in the salt, vanilla extract, and baking soda until thoroughly incorporated.

● Pour the mixture onto the parchment paper, and spread evenly with an offset spatula.

● Let cool completely, about 30 minutes. Break into pieces, and store in an airtight container.

VARIATIONS:

Honey Peanut Brittle: Replace the ½ cup corn syrup with ⅓ cup honey and 2 tablespoons corn syrup.

Cayenne Peanut Brittle: Add ½ teaspoon cayenne pepper with the peanuts.

Tip: *Use a pastry brush to paint the backs of shards of peanut brittle with tempered chocolate (page 20) or melted chocolate coating for a special treat.*

Rocky Road Chocolate Bark

MAKES ABOUT $1\frac{1}{2}$ *pounds*

I put this recipe in the Crunchy chapter, but the truth is that Rocky Road Chocolate Bark is crunchy, chewy, and silky all at the same time! It's also delicious. Once you learn to make this recipe, you'll be ready to experiment with countless chocolate bark variations.

METHOD

● Line a baking sheet with parchment paper.

● Scatter the marshmallows onto the parchment paper, over an area of about 10 x 14 inches. Pour on the tempered chocolate, and spread it evenly with an offset spatula. Sprinkle with the almonds and the salt, if using. Let the bark sit undisturbed until set. Break into irregular pieces, and store in an airtight container.

VARIATIONS:

Think of chocolate bark as a blank tablet with endless pages on which to experiment. It's easy to create your own combinations of colors, flavors, and textures. Just use the same proportions as in the main recipe and have fun trying different ingredients. Here are a couple of ideas to get you started.

Fruit & Nut Bark: Dark, milk, or white chocolate with ¾ cup roasted nuts (page 134) and ¾ cup dried fruit or candied ginger (page 136).

Cookies & Cream Bark: White chocolate with approximately 12 chopped chocolate-and-cream sandwich cookies.

Tips: *If you find yourself with leftover tempered chocolate, use it to make chocolate bark by simply pouring the chocolate onto parchment paper and sprinkling with your favorite toppings.*

Mix ingredients that need to be stored airtight (such as marshmallows and chocolate-and-cream sandwich cookies) into the chocolate rather than sprinkling them on top.

YOU WILL NEED

Baking sheet
Parchment paper
Offset spatula

¾ cup vanilla marshmallows (page 116), chopped, or ¾ cup miniature marshmallows

1 pound (1½ cups) dark, milk, or white chocolate, tempered (page 20), or 1 pound coating chocolate, melted

¾ cup almonds, roasted (page 134)

Flakey sea salt or fleur de sel, for sprinkling (optional)

Chocolate-Covered Cereal Clusters

MAKES ABOUT ¾ pound

Oh, come on—indulge in a little decadence. Why have cereal in milk when you can eat it in milk chocolate, or even dark chocolate? Crisp, light cereal and a flavorful accompaniment work very well. I suggest cornflakes and raisins, crisped rice and dried tart cherries, and oat O's and toffee.

METHOD

● Line a baking sheet with parchment paper.

● Mix together all of the ingredients with a large spoon. With gloved hands or two spoons, place small mounds of the mixture on the parchment paper. Work quickly so that the chocolate does not set up in the bowl. Let sit undisturbed until set. Store in an airtight container.

VARIATION:

PB & J Clusters: Mix together 5 ounces milk chocolate and ¼ cup peanut butter. Add 1 cup roasted peanuts and ½ cup chopped dried (not freeze-dried) strawberries. You'll be amazed by how much this tastes like the sandwich!

YOU WILL NEED

Baking sheet

Parchment paper

Large spoon

Food-safe gloves or 2 spoons

¾ cup cereal

¾ cup dried fruit or toffee, chopped

4 ounces dark, milk, or white chocolate, tempered (page 20), or chocolate coating, melted

Salted Chocolate Caramel Lollipops

MAKES ABOUT 20 lollipops

If you like the delicious combination of salt, chocolate, and caramel together, you'll love how these lollipops prolong the sensation.

→ YOU WILL NEED

METHOD

● If you don't have lollipop molds, place a silicone mat on a baking sheet.

● Boil the corn syrup, butter, kosher salt, and cream in a 1-quart saucepan over medium heat. Meanwhile, caramelize the sugar (page 34) over medium-high heat with a heatproof spatula in a 2-quart saucepan. When the sugar is caramelized, immediately reduce the heat to low, and add the cream mixture, scraping the pan. Stir over medium-high heat until the mixture is smooth. Add the chocolate. Cook to 274°F, stirring slowly and constantly.

● Remove from the heat, and quickly drop the syrup from the tip of a large spoon into the cavities of the lollipop molds, if using. Alternatively, drop the syrup onto the silicone mat so that it forms 2-inch disks, placed to leave space for the sticks. Place a lollipop stick in the center of each disk, and twist it 180° so that it is fully covered in syrup. Sprinkle the salt on top, crushing it between your fingers so that it's not too jagged. Let cool completely. Peel off the lollipops, and store in an airtight container.

Tip: *If you've got the patience, you can drop the syrup into small dots for free-form hard candies instead.*

YOU WILL NEED

Lollipop molds or silicone mat and baking sheet

1-quart saucepan

Heatproof silicone spatula

2-quart saucepan

Candy thermometer

Large spoon

Lollipop sticks

1	tablespoon corn syrup
1	tablespoon butter
¾	teaspoon kosher salt
½	cup cream
1	cup sugar
1½	ounces chocolate, chopped
	Flakey sea salt, for sprinkling

Coffee Lollipops

MAKES ABOUT 16 lollipops

You may feel as if you're experimenting with a chemistry set as you make these irresistible lollipops. The syrup will foam briskly, but all of the bubbles will disappear as it cools to leave you with lollipops as clear as a fresh pot of coffee.

METHOD

● If you don't have lollipop molds, place a silicone mat on a baking sheet.

● Boil all ingredients over medium heat to 280°F in a 2-quart saucepan, stirring occasionally with the spatula. Remove from the heat, and quickly drop the syrup from the tip of a large spoon into the cavities of the lollipop molds, if using. Alternatively, drop the syrup onto the silicone mat so that it forms 2-inch disks, placed to leave space for the sticks. Place a lollipop stick in the center of each disk, and twist it 180° so that it's fully covered in syrup. Let cool completely. Peel off the lollipops, and store in an airtight container.

Tips: *Don't use parchment paper instead of a silicone mat. If you do, the bubbles in the syrup won't disappear as the candy sets.*

For a clever gift to a coffee-lover, wrap the tops of the lollipops in cellophane and ribbon, and then present the pops in the kind of coffee bag that has a window.

Lollipop molds or silicone mat and baking sheet

2-quart saucepan

Candy thermometer

Heatproof silicone spatula

Large spoon

Lollipop sticks

½ cup coffee

¾ cup plus 2 tablespoons sugar

3 tablespoons corn syrup

⅛ teaspoon kosher salt

Liquor Lollipops

MAKES ABOUT 16 lollipops

While these lollipops are quick to make, you need to wait a day for their flavor to develop—the subtle and intriguing results are worth it. Lollipop molds make the process quicker, but you can also use a baking sheet and silicone mat instead.

→ YOU WILL NEED

METHOD

● If you don't have lollipop molds, place a silicone mat on a baking sheet.

● Mix together ¼ cup of the liquor, and the water, sugar, corn syrup, and salt in a 2-quart saucepan until all of the sugar is wet. If sugar crystals cling to the sides of the pan, dissolve them away with a wet pastry brush.

● Bring the mixture to a boil over medium heat, stirring occasionally and gently with a heatproof spatula until all of the sugar is dissolved. Then boil to 300°F without stirring.

● Remove from the heat, and mix in the remaining 1 teaspoon liquor and food coloring, if using. Quickly drop the syrup from the tip of a large spoon into the cavities of the lollipop molds, if using. Alternatively, drop the syrup onto the silicone mat so that it forms 2-inch disks, placed to leave space for the sticks. Place a lollipop stick in the center of each disk, and twist it 180° so that it's fully covered in syrup. Let cool completely. Peel off the lollipops, and store in an airtight container.

Tip: *Beautifully presented lollipops in an array of flavors make a creative gift for a liquor aficionado.*

YOU WILL NEED

Lollipop molds or silicone mat and baking sheet

2-quart saucepan

Pastry brush

Candy thermometer

Heatproof silicone spatula

Large spoon

Lollipop sticks

¼ cup plus 1 teaspoon hard liquor, such as bourbon, tequila, or rum, divided

2 tablespoons water

¾ cup sugar

3 tablespoons corn syrup

⅛ teaspoon kosher salt

¼ teaspoon food coloring of choice (optional)

Honeycomb Candy

MAKES ABOUT 1½ pounds

Not only is this candy a wonder to make because of the way it foams up majestically after the baking soda is added, it's also a wonder to eat because of its light, airy crispiness.

→

Baking sheet

Parchment paper

2-quart saucepan

Pastry brush

Heatproof silicone spatula

Serrated knife

¼ cup water

1 cup sugar

¼ cup corn syrup

2 teaspoons baking soda, sifted

2 pounds milk or dark chocolate, tempered (page 20), or coating chocolate

METHOD

● Line a baking sheet with parchment paper.

● Mix together the water, sugar, and corn syrup in a 2-quart saucepan without stirring. If sugar crystals cling to the sides of the pan, dissolve them away with a wet pastry brush.

● Boil over medium-high heat without stirring until the syrup just turns golden. Add the baking soda. Stir thoroughly and vigorously with a heatproof spatula.

● Pour onto the parchment paper, and let cool without disturbing. Once cool, use a long serrated knife to cut honeycomb into 2-inch long pieces. (It's okay if they're not exactly 2 inches long.) Holding each piece between your thumb and forefinger, dip halfway into the tempered chocolate, letting excess chocolate drip back into the bowl. Place on parchment paper to set, and then store in an airtight container.

Meringues

MAKES ABOUT 60 meringues

I love how the batter for meringues billows up when whisked and then the individual pieces turn crunchy after drying in the oven. You'll love how these meringues dissolve like air on your tongue.

→ YOU WILL NEED

METHOD

● Preheat the oven to 250°F.

● Line two baking sheets with parchment paper.

● In the bowl of the stand mixer, whisk the egg whites on medium speed until foamy. Add the cream of tartar and salt. Whisk on high speed until soft peaks form. Gradually add the sugar, about a table-spoon at a time, waiting until it's incorporated before adding more. Add the vanilla extract. Whisk until stiff peaks form. Stop whisking, and add food coloring, if using, then mix on low to incorporate.

● Drop the meringue by teaspoonfuls onto the baking sheets or pipe small kisses with a pastry bag fitted with a star tip.

● Bake at 250°F until dry, 40 to 45 minutes. Let cool before removing from the baking sheets.

Tip: *Divide the meringue between different bowls before adding the coloring to make an assortment of different colors from one batch.*

YOU WILL NEED

2 baking sheets

Parchment paper

5-quart stand mixer

Pastry bag (optional)

Star tip for piping (optional)

½ cup egg whites (about 4 large egg whites)

¼ teaspoon cream of tartar

Pinch salt

1 cup sugar

1 teaspoon vanilla extract (page 130)

Liquid food coloring, 3 to 5 drops (optional)

Candied Apples

MAKES 8 apples

Candied apples can make the unique confectionery claim of being crunchy, chewy, and juicy all in the same bite. They're also surprisingly easy and fun to make at home.

Baking sheet
Parchment paper
8 wooden craft sticks
2-quart saucepan
Heatproof silicone spatula
Candy thermometer

8 medium apples
3 cups sugar
½ cup water
½ cup corn syrup
1 drop cinnamon oil (optional)
1 teaspoon red food coloring (optional)

METHOD

● Line a baking sheet with parchment paper.

● Insert a wooden craft stick into the stem end of each apple.

● Bring the sugar, water, and corn syrup to a boil over medium-high heat in a 2-quart saucepan, stirring with a heatproof spatula until the sugar dissolves. Then cook to 300°F without stirring.

● Remove from the heat, and stir in the cinnamon oil and food coloring, if using. Let the saucepan rest off the heat until the bubbles disappear from the syrup.

● Quickly dip the apples in the syrup, and then swirl gently above the pan so the excess syrup streams off. Place on parchment paper to cool completely.

Tip: *If the syrup gets too thick in the pan, gently reheat it over low heat to thin it out.*

VARIATION:

Spirited Candied Apples: For candied apples for adults, decrease the water to 2 tablespoons, and add 1 cup whisky, bourbon, or rum with the sugar.

Sour Cream Candied Nuts

MAKES ABOUT 2 cups

This charmingly old-fashioned recipe makes nuts that are enrobed in a thick, sugary coating and infused with an alluring spiciness.

METHOD

● Line a baking sheet with parchment paper.

● Use a wooden spoon to combine the sugar, salt, and sour cream in a 2-quart saucepan. Stir occasionally over medium heat until the mixture reaches 240°F.

● Remove from the heat. Add the vanilla, cinnamon, and nuts to the syrup, and stir vigorously until the syrup becomes dry and matted, 3 to 5 minutes.

● Pour the coated nuts onto the parchment paper, and immediately separate the nuts using gloved hands. Let cool, and store in an airtight container.

YOU WILL NEED

Baking sheet

Parchment paper

Wooden spoon

2-quart saucepan

Candy thermometer

Food-safe gloves

⅔ cup packed dark brown sugar

½ teaspoon kosher salt

¼ cup sour cream

¾ teaspoon vanilla extract (page 130)

1½ teaspoons cinnamon

1¼ cups walnuts, almonds, and/or pecans, roasted (page 134)

Sweet & Salty Snack Tray

MAKES ENOUGH TO SERVE *about 6 snackers*

If you're having friends over to watch a big game, this array of treats has it all: salty, sweet, crunchy, spicy, and tangy. Individually wrapped in cellophane and presented in a decorative tin, these snacks would also make a much appreciated gift.

METHOD

CHOCOLATE-DIPPED POTATO CHIPS AND PRETZELS

● Line a baking sheet with parchment paper.

● With gloved hands, dip the potato chips halfway in the tempered chocolate, shaking to remove any excess. Place on parchment paper to set. Repeat with the pretzels.

CARAMEL CORN

● Preheat oven to 225°F. Pour popcorn and roasted nuts, if using, into a roasting pan.

● Combine sugars, water, butter, cream, corn syrup, molasses, and salt in a 2-quart saucepan. Cook over medium heat, stirring occasionally with a heatproof silicone spatula, until the mixture reaches 250°F.

(continued)

Baking sheet

Parchment paper

Food-safe gloves

Roasting pan

2-quart saucepan

Heatproof silicone spatula

Candy thermometer

SOUR CREAM CANDIED NUTS (PAGE 58)

CHOCOLATE-DIPPED POTATO CHIPS AND PRETZELS

1 bag (5 ounces) ridged potato chips

1 bag (7 ounces) thin pretzels

1 pound dark or milk chocolate, tempered (page 20)

CARAMEL CORN

10 cups popped popcorn, unsalted and unbuttered

1 cup roasted nuts, such as peanuts or almonds (page 134) (optional)

½ cup firmly packed dark brown sugar

½ cup sugar

2 tablespoons water

6 tablespoons unsalted butter

2 tablespoons cream

2 tablespoons corn syrup

1 tablespoon molasses

½ teaspoon salt

¼ teaspoon baking soda

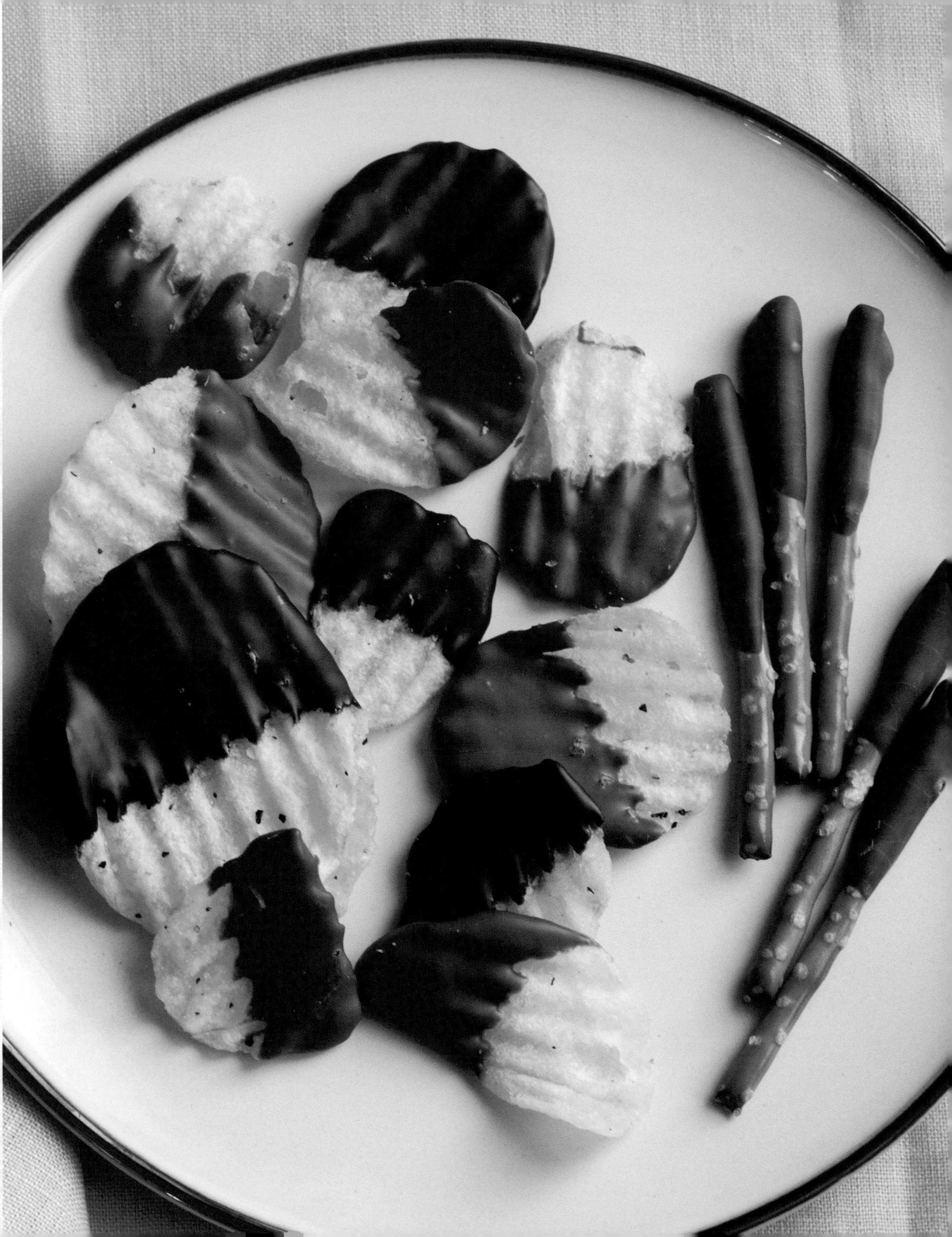

● Remove from the heat. Stir in the baking soda, and mix thoroughly to incorporate.

● Pour the syrup over the popcorn, and stir until popcorn is coated. Bake for 45 minutes, stirring every 15 minutes. The caramel corn is done when it's dry and crispy when cool. Store in an airtight container.

VARIATION:

Orange Cashew Caramel Corn:
Add 1 cup roasted cashews (page 134) to the popcorn, and the zest of 1 orange (1 packed teaspoon) with the cream. Boil to 254°F instead of 250°F. Add 2 teaspoons soy sauce with the baking soda.

Above:
Caramel Corn

Below:
Orange Cashew
Caramel Corn

Crystallized Flowers

MAKES 30 pieces

Crystallized flowers are an elegant and edible candy garnish for cakes, pastries, or truffles.

METHOD

● Whisk the egg whites in a small bowl until foamy. Place the sugar in a small bowl.

● Use a small paintbrush to apply the egg white evenly and thoroughly onto one flower. Using tweezers, pick up the flower by its base, and hold it above the bowl of sugar while using a spoon to sprinkle sugar onto it.

● Place the flower on a cooling rack, and repeat until all flowers are coated. Let dry completely, at least overnight. Store in an airtight container.

Tip: *If you don't have superfine sugar, you may process granulated sugar in batches in a clean coffee grinder.*

YOU WILL NEED

Whisk

2 small bowls

Small paintbrush

Tweezers

Spoon

Cooling rack

2 egg whites

2 cups superfine sugar

30 edible, unsprayed flowers, such as pansies, violets, or roses

Chewy Candy

Vanilla Caramels

*MAKES **64** pieces*

These are soft and silky caramels, designed to melt in your mouth while bursting with the full flavors of vanilla and caramel.

YOU WILL NEED

METHOD

● Line an 8 x 8-inch baking pan with plastic wrap.

● Bring the corn syrup, butter, kosher salt, cream, and vanilla seeds and pod to a boil in a 1-quart saucepan over medium heat, and then decrease heat to low.

● Meanwhile, caramelize the sugar in a 2-quart pot using the method described on page 34. When the sugar has fully caramelized, turn off the heat. Slowly add the cream mixture into the caramelized sugar, being careful of splatter.

● Stir the syrup constantly and gently on medium-high heat, until it reaches 250°F.

● Pour into the prepared pan, and cover with plastic wrap. Let set overnight at room temperature.

● Unwrap the caramel and place on a cutting board covered with parchment paper. (This will keep the caramel from sticking to the cutting board and also keep any odors from transferring from the board to the candy.) Use a chef's knife or pizza wheel to cut the slab into ½-inch wide strips, and cut each strip into 2-inch long pieces. Wrap each piece individually in cellophane or waxed paper.

VARIATION:

Chocolate Caramels: Omit the vanilla. Add 3 ounces chopped dark chocolate to the syrup after the cream has been incorporated into the sugar. Boil to 247°F.

8 x 8-inch baking pan

Plastic wrap

1-quart saucepan

2-quart saucepan

Heatproof silicone spatula

Candy thermometer

Cutting board

Parchment paper

Chef's knife or pizza wheel

Cellophane squares or waxed paper

2   tablespoons corn syrup

4   tablespoons butter, cut into cubes

1   teaspoon kosher salt

1   cup cream

1   vanilla bean, scraped, seeds and pods reserved

2   cups sugar

Pumpkin Caramels

MAKES 64 pieces

This is a pumpkin pie transformed into candy—hold the crust! If you can't find golden syrup at your grocery store, you can use molasses instead.

→ YOU WILL NEED

METHOD

● Line an 8 x 8-inch pan with plastic wrap.

● Mix together the corn syrup, golden syrup, cinnamon, ginger, and allspice into a paste in a 1-quart saucepan. Add the butter, kosher salt, and cream, and cook over medium heat. Once it comes to a boil, decrease the heat to low to keep it warm.

● Meanwhile, caramelize the sugar in a 2-quart saucepan using the method described on page 34. When the sugar has fully caramelized, turn off the heat. Slowly add the cream mixture into the sugar, being careful of splatter. Return heat to medium high, and stir until smooth. Add the pumpkin to the syrup, and stir the syrup constantly and gently until it reaches 248°F.

● Pour into the prepared pan, and cover with plastic wrap. Let set overnight at room temperature.

● Unwrap the caramel and place it on a cutting board covered with parchment paper. (This will keep the caramel from sticking to the cutting board and also keep any odors from transferring from the board to the candy.) Use a chef's knife or pizza wheel to cut the slab into ½-inch wide strips, and cut each strip into 2-inch long pieces. Individually wrap in cellophane or waxed paper.

YOU WILL NEED

8 x 8-inch baking pan

Plastic wrap

1-quart saucepan

2-quart saucepan

Heatproof silicone spatula

Candy thermometer

Cutting board

Parchment paper

Chef's knife or pizza wheel

Cellophane squares or waxed paper

1 tablespoon corn syrup

1 tablespoon golden syrup or molasses

½ teaspoon cinnamon

¼ teaspoon ginger

⅛ teaspoon allspice

1 tablespoon butter

1¼ teaspoons kosher salt

1½ cups cream

2 cups sugar

½ cup pureed pumpkin, canned or fresh

Saltwater Taffy

MAKES ABOUT 2 pounds

This taffy may seem like hard candy when you first pop it in your mouth, but it will quickly soften and become unabashedly chewy.

METHOD

● Place the silicone mats on the counter.

● Combine the sugar and cornstarch in a 3-quart saucepan. Add the corn syrup, water, butter, and salt, and stir to combine with a heatproof spatula. Wash down any crystals on the side of the pan with a moistened pastry brush. Bring the syrup to a boil over medium heat, stirring gently only until the sugar dissolves.

● Without stirring, cook the syrup to 258°F. Remove from the heat, and stir in the baking soda.

● Pour equal amounts of the syrup onto each silicone mat. Pour a few drops of flavoring and coloring in the center of each slab, then let the taffy sit until it's cool enough to handle.

● With gloved hands, grab the taffy edges and pull into a long strand, fold the strand back together, and repeat until the taffy is glossy and firm enough to hold its shape when placed down, about 5 to 10 minutes. Roll taffy into a ½-inch-thick rope and cut into 1-inch lengths. Repeat with all slabs. Wrap each piece in a 3 x 4-inch piece of waxed paper.

Tip: *If you make more than one color of taffy from the same batch, try pulling two different colored strands together while twisting to make striped taffy.*

YOU WILL NEED

Silicone non-stick mats
(1 for each flavor or color
of taffy you are making)

3-quart saucepan

Heatproof silicone spatula

Pastry brush

Candy thermometer

Food-safe gloves

Chef's knife

Waxed paper

2 cups sugar

2 tablespoons cornstarch

1 cup light corn syrup

¾ cup water

2 tablespoons butter

¼ teaspoon salt

⅛ teaspoon baking soda

Flavoring extract (such as lime, lemon, or cherry)

Food coloring, assorted colors

Pecan Pie Taffy

MAKES ABOUT $1^1/_4$ *pounds*

If you've never made taffy, I can't imagine a better recipe with which to start. You'll marvel at how a dark brown puddle of cooked sugar transforms into a shiny golden rope in your hands. And your reward will taste just like pecan pie!

METHOD

● Coat a 9 x 13-inch baking pan with oil.

● Bring the sugars, molasses, water, and bourbon, if using, to a boil in a 3-quart saucepan over medium heat, stirring occasionally with a heatproof spatula.

● Cook to 250°F, stirring constantly and gently to prevent scorching.

● Remove from the heat. Add the butter, baking soda, salt, and vanilla, stirring just to incorporate thoroughly.

● Pour into the baking pan and sprinkle on the pecans. Let cool until it is just warm, about 30 minutes.

● With gloved or buttered hands, gather the taffy from the edges and pull until it is lightly colored and firm enough to hold its shape. Roll the taffy into a thin rope and cut it into 1-inch lengths. Wrap in waxed paper.

YOU WILL NEED

9 x 13-inch baking pan

3-quart saucepan

Heatproof silicone spatula

Candy thermometer

Food-safe gloves (optional)

Chef's knife

Waxed paper

Oil for the pan

½ cup sugar

⅓ cup packed dark brown sugar

1 cup light molasses

½ cup water

¼ cup bourbon (optional)

2 tablespoons butter

1/16 teaspoon baking soda

⅛ teaspoon kosher salt

1 teaspoon vanilla extract (page 130)

⅔ cup pecans, roasted and chopped (page 134)

Jelly Candies

MAKES ABOUT 64 pieces

Have fun experimenting with colors to match the flavors of these delightfully chewy jellies.

METHOD

● Line an 8 x 8-inch baking pan with plastic wrap, and coat with oil.

● Combine the sugar and gelatin in a 5-quart pan. Add water and bring to a boil over medium heat, stirring occasionally with a heatproof spatula. Slowly pour in the corn syrup, and return to a gentle boil. Stir the syrup constantly until it reaches 228°F.

● Remove from the heat, and thoroughly stir in the coloring, flavoring, and citric acid. Pour the syrup into the prepared pan. Let cool to room temperature.

● Cover with an oiled piece of plastic wrap and place in the freezer until firm, 1 to 2 hours. Unmold and unwrap the slab onto oiled parchment paper on a cutting board. With a chef's knife, cut jellies into 1-inch squares, and toss in sugar to coat. Store in an airtight container.

8 x 8-inch baking pan

Plastic wrap

5-quart pan

Heatproof silicone spatula

Candy thermometer

Parchment paper

Cutting board

Chef's knife

Oil for the pan

1½ cups sugar

4 tablespoons (4 envelopes) unflavored gelatin

2 cups water

1¼ cups corn syrup

¼ teaspoon liquid food coloring

1 teaspoon flavoring, such as cherry, cinnamon, or mint

¼ teaspoon citric acid

Sugar, for coating

Applesauce Jellies

MAKES ABOUT 2 pounds

As these jellies cook, the sugar caramelizes just enough to make them reminiscent of the autumnal thrill of caramel apples.

METHOD

● Line an 8 x 8-inch baking pan with plastic wrap and coat evenly with oil.

● Combine sour cream and 1¼ cups of the applesauce in a small bowl. Sprinkle the gelatin on top, and stir until smooth.

● Boil the remaining 1 cup of applesauce and the sugar over medium heat in a 3-quart saucepan, stirring occasionally with a heatproof spatula until the sugar dissolves. Add the gelatin mixture in several additions, stirring to dissolve between each. Stir the boiling mixture constantly and gently until it reaches 224°F, about 25 minutes.

● Remove from the heat, and let sit 5 minutes. Stir in the walnuts, if using, vanilla, and salt, and pour into the prepared baking pan. Let cool until room temperature, and then refrigerate overnight.

● Cut into 1-inch squares with a chef's knife. Roll in the cornstarch or powdered sugar. Store in an airtight container.

VARIATION:

Cinnamon Applesauce Jellies: Add 1½ teaspoons cinnamon to the gelatin mixture.

→ YOU WILL NEED

8 x 8-inch baking pan

Plastic wrap

Small bowl

3-quart saucepan

Heatproof silicone spatula

Candy thermometer

Chef's knife

Oil for the pan

2 tablespoons sour cream

2¼ cups applesauce, divided

3 tablespoons (3 envelopes) unflavored gelatin

2¾ cups sugar

⅔ cup walnuts, coarsely chopped (optional)

1¼ teaspoons vanilla extract (page 130)

Pinch salt

2 cups cornstarch or powdered sugar for coating

Fruit Jam Jellies

*MAKES **64** pieces*

Any flavor of jam you happen to have in your pantry will work to make these simple, delicious candies.

→ YOU WILL NEED

METHOD

● Oil an 8 x 8-inch baking pan.

● Combine the jam, water, sugar, gelatin, and citric acid in a 3-quart saucepan. Stir constantly and slowly over medium-high heat with a heatproof spatula until the syrup reaches 220°F. Pour into the prepared pan, and skim off any foam with a spoon. Let cool to room temperature, and then refrigerate until firm, about 3 hours.

● Combine the powdered sugar and cornstarch in a bowl. Unmold the jelly onto a cutting board lined with parchment paper. Cut into 1-inch squares and roll in the powdered sugar and cornstarch mixture. Store in an airtight container.

YOU WILL NEED

8 x 8-inch baking pan

3-quart saucepan

Heatproof silicone spatula

Candy thermometer

Spoon

Bowl

Cutting board

Parchment paper

Oil for the pan

1½ cups jam

¾ cup waler

¾ cup sugar

3 tablespoons (3 envelopes) unflavored gelatin

¼ teaspoon citric acid

⅓ cup powdered sugar

⅓ cup cornstarch

Blueberry Coconut Nougat

MAKES ABOUT *128* *pieces*

Nougat may seem intimidating, but it's really just sugar syrup that's whipped into egg whites, like a thick meringue. The key is to have everything ready when you start because ingredients are added at crucial times. Also, keep in mind that the nougat will need to set overnight.

METHOD

● Line a baking sheet with one silicone mat.

● Place the egg whites in the mixing bowl of a 5-quart stand mixer.

● Boil the water, sugar, corn syrup, honey, and kosher salt in a 2-quart saucepan on medium-high heat to 250°F without stirring.

● Immediately whisk the egg whites until foamy and add the powdered sugar. Whisk until soft peaks form.

● When the sugar syrup reaches 268°F, remove from the heat, and slowly pour the syrup down the inside edge of the bowl of whisked egg whites, while whisking by hand to incorporate. Place the bowl in the mixer with the whisk attachment. Mix on the highest speed for 5 minutes. Decrease to low and add the melted cocoa butter down the side of the bowl. Increase mixing speed to high, and mix to incorporate, about 30 seconds. Turn off the mixer and add the coconut. Mix on low speed until incorporated, about 30 seconds.

● Use a rubber spatula to scoop and spread the warm nougat into a ½-inch thick layer on the silicone mat that's on the baking sheet. The nougat will be about 8 x 16 inches. Immediately cover with the

YOU WILL NEED →

Baking sheet

2 silicone mats

5-quart stand mixer with whisk attachment

2-quart saucepan

Candy thermometer

Whisk

Rubber spatula

Plastic wrap

Offset spatula

Cutting board

Parchment paper

Ruler or straightedge

Pizza wheel

Dipping forks

2 egg whites

¼ cup water

1½ cups sugar

½ cup corn syrup

½ cup honey

Pinch kosher salt

2½ teaspoons powdered sugar

1 ounce cocoa butter, melted

¾ cup finely shredded dried coconut, unsweetened

2 pounds dark chocolate, tempered (page 20) or coating chocolate, melted

½ cup dried blueberries

second silicone mat. When cool, wrap the entire assemblage (baking sheet, silicone mat, nougat, and second silicone mat) in plastic wrap. Let set overnight at room temperature.

● Unwrap the assemblage, and peel the top silicone mat off the nougat. Use the offset spatula to spread tempered chocolate in a thin layer on the top of the nougat slab. Let set, and flip the slab, chocolate side down, onto a cutting board covered with parchment paper. Peel off the second silicone mat, and spread a thin layer of tempered chocolate on the second side of the nougat. Keep the leftover chocolate at temperature for dipping. Use the ruler or straightedge and pizza wheel to cut the nougat into 1-inch squares. Dip the squares in the reserved tempered chocolate according to the instructions on page 27. Depending on the size of the dried blueberries, place 1 to 3 blueberries on top of each piece before the chocolate sets. Store in an airtight container.

Caramel Pinwheels

*MAKES ABOUT **128** pieces*

These eye-catching candies let you mix flavors of caramels in a unique way. Once you've got the technique down, experiment with different flavor combinations.

YOU WILL NEED

METHOD

● Place the slab of chocolate caramel on a piece of plastic wrap. Use the palm of your hand to push down and outward on the caramel so that it thins and elongates into a slab that's about 8 x 16 inches. Repeat with the other slab of caramel on another piece of plastic wrap.

● Carefully place one slab of caramel atop the other on a cutting board covered with parchment paper. (This will keep the caramel from sticking to the cutting board and also keep any odors from transferring from the board to the candy.) Use a pizza wheel to cut this double slab of caramel in half lengthwise into two 4-inch-wide slabs. Starting at one of the long edges of a slab, roll the caramel tightly into a log shape. Repeat with the remaining slab.

● Use a chef's knife to cut each log into two pieces. With your fingers extended, roll each log, one at a time, in the palms of your hands until it elongates and becomes thinner, about 1 inch in diameter. Cut each log into 1-inch pieces, and wrap in cellophane.

YOU WILL NEED

Plastic wrap

Cutting board

Parchment paper

Pizza wheel

Chef's knife

Cellophane squares

8 x 8-inch slab of chocolate caramel (page 69)

8 x 8-inch slab of vanilla (or pumpkin) caramel (page 68 or 70)

Orange Walnut Chocolate Nougat

MAKES 128 pieces

In some ways, this nougat is like a tricked-out brownie—chocolaty, chewy, nutty, and intriguingly spiked with orange.

YOU WILL NEED

METHOD

- Line a baking sheet with one silicone mat.

- Place the egg whites in the mixing bowl of a 5-quart stand mixer.

- Boil the water, sugar, corn syrup, honey, and kosher salt in a 2-quart saucepan on medium-high heat to 250°F without stirring.

- Immediately whisk the egg whites until foamy and add the powdered sugar. Whisk until soft peaks form.

- When the sugar syrup reaches 270°F, remove from the heat, and slowly pour the syrup down the inside edge of the bowl of whisked egg whites, while whisking by hand to incorporate. Place the bowl in the mixer with the whisk attachment. Mix on the highest speed for 5 minutes. Decrease to low and add the melted unsweetened chocolate down the side of the bowl. Increase to high speed and mix to incorporate, about 30 seconds. Turn off the mixer and add the walnuts. Mix on low speed until incorporated, about 30 seconds.

- Use a rubber spatula to scoop and spread the warm nougat into a ½-inch thick layer on the silicone mat that's on the baking sheet. The nougat will be about 8 x 16 inches. Immediately cover with the second silicone mat. When cool, wrap the entire assemblage (baking sheet, silicone mat, nougat, and second silicone mat) in plastic wrap. Let set overnight at room temperature.

- Unwrap the assemblage, and peel the top silicone mat off the nougat. Use the offset spatula to spread tempered chocolate in a thin layer on the top of the nougat slab. Let set, and flip the slab, chocolate side down, onto a cutting board covered with parchment paper. Peel off the second silicone mat, and spread a thin layer of tempered chocolate on the second side of the nougat. Keep the leftover chocolate at temperature for dipping. Use the ruler or straightedge and pizza wheel to cut the nougat into 1-inch squares. Dip according to the instructions on page 27. Press a piece of candied orange peel on top of each piece before the chocolate sets for garnish. Store in an airtight container.

Baking sheet

2 silicone mats

5-quart stand mixer with whisk attachment

2-quart saucepan

Candy thermometer

Whisk

Rubber spatula

Plastic wrap

Offset spatula

Cutting board

Parchment paper

Ruler or straightedge

Pizza wheel

Dipping forks

2 egg whites

¼ cup water

1½ cups sugar

½ cup corn syrup

½ cup honey

Pinch kosher salt

2½ teaspoons powdered sugar

2 ounces unsweetened chocolate, melted

1 cup walnuts, roasted and finely chopped (page 134)

2 pounds tempered dark chocolate (page 20) or melting chocolate

64 pieces of candied orange peel (page 132), ½ inch each

Peach Turkish Delights

MAKES 64 pieces

The luscious texture of Turkish delights is the perfect platform for a peach candy. The roasted almonds complement the flavor and diffuse the sweetness.

METHOD

● Line an 8 x 8-inch pan with plastic wrap and coat with oil.

● Combine ½ cup of the water, the sugar, and the lemon juice in a 1-quart saucepan, and boil to 260°F over medium-high heat without stirring. Remove from the heat.

● Whisk together the cornstarch, cream of tartar, and 1½ cups of the water in a 3-quart saucepan. Bring to a boil over medium heat, and whisk for 5 minutes. It will be very thick.

● Add half of the sugar syrup to the cornstarch mixture, and whisk to incorporate. Add the remaining half, and whisk to incorporate. Continue whisking on medium-low heat until smooth and clear, about 20 to 25 minutes.

● Remove from the heat, and whisk in peach flavoring, colorings, and almonds. Pour into the prepared pan, and let cool to room temperature. Cover pan in plastic wrap, and let set overnight at room temperature.

● Cut into 1-inch pieces, and roll in powdered sugar to coat. Store in an airtight container.

YOU WILL NEED

8 x 8-inch baking pan

Plastic wrap

1-quart saucepan

Candy thermometer

Whisk

3-quart saucepan

Chef's knife

Oil for the pan

2 cups water, divided

2 cups sugar

1 teaspoon lemon juice

½ cup cornstarch

½ teaspoon cream of tartar

1 teaspoon peach flavoring

1 drop orange coloring

1 drop yellow coloring

½ cup almonds, roasted and coarsely chopped (page 134)

½ cup powdered sugar

Sugarplums

MAKES ABOUT $^{1}/_{2}$ *pound*

If you've ever had visions of sugarplums dancing in your head (and who hasn't?), you'll enjoy making these delectable holiday treats. They come together in a snap, and their flavor continues to develop over time.

METHOD

● In a medium bowl, combine the sugar, allspice, cardamom, and cinnamon.

● Use a food processor to finely chop the pistachios and almonds. Transfer the chopped nuts to a bowl, and reserve.

● In the food processor, chop the plums, dates, apricots, and honey until they just begin to clump. Add the reserved nuts and the rosewater, and process until the mixture forms a ball.

● Transfer the mixture to a clean bowl, and roll into 1-inch diameter balls. Roll each ball in the sugar and spice mixture to cover completely, and store in the refrigerator in an airtight container.

Tip: *Dried plums look like flattened halves of plums. They are more tart and flavorful than prunes. If dried plums are unavailable, use dried figs instead.*

YOU WILL NEED

3 bowls

Food processor

½ cup sugar

¼ teaspoon allspice

¼ teaspoon cardamom

¼ teaspoon cinnamon

¼ cup pistachios, roasted (page 134)

½ cup almonds, roasted (page 134)

1 cup dried plums (not prunes)

1 cup dates

½ cup dried apricots

2 tablespoons honey

½ teaspoon rosewater

Silky Candy

Chocolate Fudge

MAKES ONE 8 x 8-inch slab of fudge

Luscious, silken, and an all-time champ in the candy world, this classic fudge will please every sweet tooth.

→ YOU WILL NEED

METHOD

● Oil an 8 x 8-inch baking pan.

● Bring the sugar, cream, milk, corn syrup, and salt to a boil over medium heat in a 3-quart saucepan, stirring occasionally with a heatproof spatula. Add the chocolate, and boil to 238°F, stirring frequently. Remove from the heat, and stir in the vanilla extract.

● Pour the syrup in a thin layer in a 9 x 13-inch baking pan. Let cool to 110°F undisturbed, about 20 minutes. Scrape the syrup into the bowl of a stand mixer.

● Mix on medium speed with a paddle attachment until the fudge thickens and begins to hold its shape, about 7 minutes. Scrape into the prepared 8 x 8-inch pan, and spread evenly with an offset spatula. Let set for at least 2 hours at room temperature. Cut into pieces of desired size, and store in an airtight container.

VARIATION:

Chocolate Ginger Fudge: Add ⅓ cup finely chopped candied ginger (page 136) after 2 minutes of mixing. Sprinkle with an additional ¼ cup of finely chopped candied ginger once the fudge has been spread in the 8 x 8-inch pan.

YOU WILL NEED

8 x 8-inch baking pan

3-quart saucepan

Heatproof silicone spatula

Candy thermometer

9 x 13-inch baking pan

5-quart stand mixer

Offset spatula

Chef's knife

Oil for the pan

2 cups sugar

½ cup cream

¼ cup milk

¼ cup corn syrup

¾ teaspoon kosher salt

4 ounces unsweetened chocolate, finely chopped

1½ teaspoons vanilla extract (page 130)

Vanilla Cheesecake Fudge

MAKES ONE 8-inch-diameter circular slab

Creamy, tangy, and full of vanilla, this unique fudge will satisfy any
and all cheesecake cravings. Using a round cake pan to mold the fudge
will add to the presentation.

METHOD

● Oil an 8-inch round cake pan.

● Bring the sugar, corn syrup, milk, and vanilla seeds to a boil in a
3-quart saucepan over medium heat, stirring occasionally with a
heatproof spatula. Boil to 250°F, stirring frequently. The syrup will
become a light brown color.

● Pour the mixture into a 9 x 13-inch baking pan, and let cool to 120°F,
about 20 minutes.

● Scrape the syrup into the bowl of a stand mixer, and add the cream
cheese and salt. Mix on medium speed with the paddle attachment for
15 seconds. Scrape down the sides of the mixing bowl, and then mix
on high speed until the mixture thickens slightly and begins to hold its
shape, about 10 minutes.

● Pour into the prepared cake pan, and sprinkle with the dried fruit.
Let cool to room temperature. Refrigerate overnight.

● Unmold from the pan and cut in wedge-shaped cake slices. Store in
an airtight container in the refrigerator.

Tip: *For a gift, separate slices with pieces of waxed paper to mimic a
traditional cheesecake presentation.*

YOU WILL NEED

8-inch round cake pan

3-quart saucepan

Heatproof silicone spatula

Candy thermometer

9 x 13-inch baking pan

5-quart stand mixer

Oil for the pan

4 cups sugar

½ cup corn syrup

6 ounces milk

1 vanilla bean, scraped,
seeds only

4 ounces (½ package)
cream cheese

¼ teaspoon kosher salt

⅓ cup dried fruit, such as
cherries or blueberries

Chocolate Chip Cookie Dough Fudge

MAKES ONE 8 x 8-inch slab

Penuche is a classic brown sugar fudge with ingredients almost identical to those of chocolate chip cookies. This recipe riff bridges the gap between candy and cookie with delicious results.

METHOD

● Oil an 8 x 8-inch baking pan.

● Bring the sugar, dark brown sugar, cream, milk, corn syrup, and salt to a boil over medium heat in a 3-quart saucepan, stirring occasionally with a heatproof spatula. Boil to 242°F, stirring frequently. Remove from the heat and stir in the butter, vanilla, and flour. Pour the syrup into a 9 x 13-inch baking pan in a thin layer. Let cool to 110°F undisturbed at room temperature, about 20 minutes. Scrape the syrup into the bowl of a stand mixer.

● Mix on medium speed with a paddle attachment until the fudge thickens and begins to hold its shape, 3 to 5 minutes. Scrape into the prepared 8 x 8-inch baking pan, and spread evenly with an offset spatula. Sprinkle the chocolate chips on top, then lightly press them into the fudge. Let cool and set, at least 2 hours. Chill in the fridge for about 30 minutes if the chocolate chips are still soft. Cut into pieces of desired size, and store in an airtight container.

YOU WILL NEED

8 x 8-inch baking pan

3-quart saucepan

Heatproof silicone spatula

Candy thermometer

9 x 13-inch baking pan

5-quart stand mixer

Offset spatula

Chef's knife

Oil for the pan

1¾   cups sugar

¾   cup dark brown sugar

½   cup cream

¼   cup milk

1   tablespoon corn syrup

¾   teaspoon kosher salt

2   tablespoons butter

1   teaspoon vanilla extract (page 130)

½   cup flour

⅓   cup chocolate chips

Mixed-Nut Dark Chocolate Truffles

MAKES ABOUT 35 truffles

In a perfect world, these intense shots of pure chocolate pleasure would always be waiting in the refrigerator: cool and creamy with just the right accent of nutty flavor.

Food processor

1-quart saucepan

Heatproof silicone spatula

2 stainless steel bowls

Plastic wrap

Miniature ice cream scoop or melon baller

Food-safe gloves

9	ounces dark chocolate, roughly chopped
1	tablespoon corn syrup
	Pinch kosher salt
1	cup cream
⅓	cup roasted almonds (page 134)
⅓	cup roasted pecans
⅓	cup roasted walnuts
1½	teaspoons fleur de sel or flakey sea salt

METHOD

● Use a food processor to finely chop the roughly chopped chocolate.

● Bring the corn syrup, salt, and cream to a boil over medium-high heat in a 1-quart saucepan without stirring.

● Pour the cream mixture over the chocolate, and process for 30 seconds. Scrape down the sides of the food processor bowl with a heatproof spatula. Process for 30 seconds more, or until completely smooth. Pour the mixture into a stainless steel bowl, and cover directly with plastic wrap. Refrigerate until firm, about 3 hours.

● Process the almonds, pecans, walnuts, and sea salt in the clean bowl of the food processor until finely ground, about 20 seconds. Pour the mixture into a clean stainless steel bowl. Use a miniature ice cream scoop or melon baller to form 1-inch-diameter truffles, roll each lightly by hand, and then roll each truffle in the nut mixture until fully coated. Store in an airtight container in the refrigerator.

Pear Hazelnut Truffles

MAKES 64 truffles

Pears and hazelnuts are treasures of the Pacific Northwest—the addition of chocolate makes them out of this world.

YOU WILL NEED

METHOD

● Line an 8 x 8-inch baking pan with plastic wrap.

● Use a food processor to finely chop the coarsely chopped white and milk chocolates.

● Bring the cream and salt to a boil over medium-high heat in a 1-quart saucepan. Add the pear liqueur, and immediately pour the cream mixture over the chopped chocolate. Process for 30 seconds. Scrape down the sides of the food processor bowl with a heatproof spatula. Process for 1 minute more, or until completely smooth.

● Pour the mixture into the prepared pan, and smooth the top with an offset spatula. Cover with plastic wrap and let set overnight in a cool room.

● Remove the wrapped slab from the baking pan, and place it on a cutting board. Use the offset spatula to spread a thin layer of the tempered chocolate on the slab. Let set, and then flip over onto a piece of parchment paper, and spread a thin layer of chocolate on the second side.

● Score the slab into 1-inch-square pieces with a ruler or straightedge and a pizza wheel before the chocolate sets. Cut a row at a time into squares, and dip according to the instructions on page 27. Garnish with a triangle of dried pear on one corner and a half hazelnut on the diagonal corner.

8 x 8-inch baking pan

Plastic wrap

Food processor

1-quart saucepan

Heatproof silicone spatula

Offset spatula

Cutting board

Parchment paper

Ruler or straightedge

Pizza wheel

Chef's knife

Dipping forks

10 ounces white chocolate, coarsely chopped

2 ounces milk chocolate, coarsely chopped

4 ounces cream

Pinch kosher salt

4 teaspoons pear liqueur

2 pounds milk chocolate, tempered (page 20)

64 dried pear pieces, cut into triangles with two ½-inch sides

32 hazelnuts, roasted, skinned, and cut in half (page 134)

Piña Colada Truffles

MAKES 64 truffles

Complete with a candied cherry, bits of pineapple, and coconut, these truffles will practically whisk you away to a sandy beach with your first bite.

METHOD

● Line an 8 x-8-inch baking pan with plastic wrap.

● Use a food processor to finely chop the coarsely chopped white chocolate. Bring the cream, coconut milk, and salt to a boil over medium-high heat in a 1-quart saucepan. Add the rum, and immediately pour the cream mixture over the chocolate. Process for 30 seconds. Scrape down the sides of the food processor bowl with a heatproof spatula. Process for 1 minute more, or until completely smooth. Add the candied pineapple, and process for 15 seconds more. Pour the mixture into the prepared pan and smooth the top with an offset spatula. Cover with plastic wrap and let set overnight in a cool room.

● Remove the wrapped slab from the baking pan, and place it on a cutting board. Use an offset spatula to spread a thin layer of the tempered white chocolate on the slab. Let set, and then flip over onto a piece of parchment paper, and spread a thin layer of white chocolate on the second side.

● Score the slab into 1-inch-square pieces with a ruler or straightedge and a pizza wheel before the chocolate sets. Cut a row at a time into squares, and dip according to the instructions on page 27. Garnish with coconut and a candied cherry sliver.

YOU WILL NEED

8 x 8-inch baking pan

Plastic wrap

Food processor

1-quart saucepan

Heatproof silicone spatula

Offset spatula

Cutting board

Parchment paper

Ruler or straightedge

Pizza wheel

Chef's knife

Dipping forks

12 ounces white chocolate, coarsely chopped

2 ounces cream

1 ounce coconut milk

Pinch kosher salt

1 tablespoon dark rum

¼ cup finely chopped candied pineapple, about 1 ring

2 pounds white chocolate, tempered (page 20)

½ cup finely shredded dried coconut, unsweetened

8 candied cherries, each cut into 8 slices

Divinity Sundaes

MAKES 36 pieces

Divinity is a thick meringue-like candy that is less dense and less chewy than nougat and commonly associated with the American South. Its name comes from its divinely light and airy texture, and decorating this confection like a miniature ice cream sundae just completes the delicious effect.

METHOD

● Line an 8 x 8-inch baking pan with parchment paper, and oil the parchment.

● Place the egg whites and 2 tablespoons of the sugar in the bowl of a stand mixer.

● Bring the water, 2 cups sugar, and corn syrup to a boil in a 2-quart saucepan over medium-high heat, stirring occasionally with a heatproof spatula until the sugar is dissolved. When the syrup reaches 240°F, whip the egg whites mixture on high speed to form very stiff peaks. Then whip the egg whites on low until the syrup reaches 252°F.

Tip: *If the egg whites don't stay in motion once they are whipped, they'll separate (water will collect underneath), and if they are kept on high speed, they'll also separate. It should only take a couple minutes for the syrup to reach 252°F.*

● Pour the syrup down the side of the mixer bowl containing the whipped egg whites, and mix on high. While mixing, slowly pour the vanilla extract down the side of the bowl, and continue mixing until the divinity becomes slightly dull and thick enough to completely hold its shape, about 10 minutes. Turn the mixer to low speed, and add the walnuts and kosher salt. Scrape the divinity into the prepared pan, and spread evenly with an offset spatula. Let cool at room temperature.

● Unmold the slab of divinity, and use a ruler or straightedge to cut the slab into roughly 1¼ x 1¼-inch squares. Drizzle tempered dark chocolate on top of each square so that a little runs over each edge. Sprinkle on the toppings, and place a candied cherry half on top of each square.

8 x 8-inch baking pan

Parchment paper

5-quart stand mixer

2-quart saucepan

Heatproof silicone spatula

Candy thermometer

Offset spatula

Ruler or straightedge

Chef's knife

Oil for the pan

2 large egg whites

2 tablespoons plus 2 cups sugar, divided

½ cup water

½ cup corn syrup

1 teaspoon vanilla extract (page 130)

1 cup walnuts, chopped

¼ teaspoon kosher salt

4 ounces dark chocolate, tempered (page 20) or coating chocolate, melted

⅓ cup toppings, such as sprinkles, finely chopped nuts, or coconut

18 candied cherries, cut in half

Chocolate Caramallows

*MAKES ABOUT **40** pieces*

Chocolate and vanilla are a classic pairing for a reason: Each heightens the flavor of the other, and the addition of salt—perhaps the ultimate flavor enhancer—makes for a confection that's deviously addictive.

Plastic wrap

Chef's knife

40 rectangles of parchment paper, about 6 x 4 inches each

1 slab of chocolate caramel, 8 x 8 inches (page 69)

40 vanilla marshmallows (page 116)

Flakey sea salt (optional)

METHOD

● Place the 8 x 8 slab of chocolate caramel on a large piece of plastic wrap. With the palm of your hand, push down and outward on the caramel so that it thins and elongates. Work with the caramel until it's about 8 x 20 inches.

● Use a chef's knife to cut a 1-inch-wide strip of caramel from an 8-inch end of the slab. Place a marshmallow on one end, and roll the strip of caramel around it. Cut the strip where it starts to overlap, and pinch the two ends of the caramel strip together to make the wrapping continuous. Sprinkle with salt, if desired. Wrap in parchment paper. Repeat until you run out of caramel or marshmallows.

Dot Candy

MAKES ABOUT ½ pound

These candies have a compelling crystallized texture and can be created in an array of colors and flavors. A very steady hand is required to make the small dots that we all remember from old-fashioned dot candy, so feel free to make big ones—they're just as fun and delicious.

METHOD

● Line your counter with parchment paper.

● Combine the sugar, cream, and water in a 1-quart saucepan, and stir gently. Wash down any crystals on the sides of the pan with a moistened pastry brush. Cook syrup to 240°F over medium heat without stirring.

● Remove from the heat, and with a stainless steel spoon, stir in the butter, flavoring extract, and food coloring. Stir until the syrup thickens slightly, about 1 minute, and then drop from the tip of the spoon onto the parchment paper to form the dots. Cut the parchment paper into strips.

YOU WILL NEED

Parchment paper
1-quart saucepan
Pastry brush
Candy thermometer
Stainless steel spoon

1 cup sugar

3 tablespoons cream

2 tablespoons water

1 teaspoon butter

5 drops flavoring extract, such as mint, cherry, or lemon

3 drops food coloring, such as blue, red, or yellow

Peanut Butter & Maple Pralines

MAKES ABOUT 35 pieces

Move over, peanut butter and jelly. Peanut butter and maple syrup are a combination to be reckoned with—as you'll discover when you bite into one of these unique candies.

METHOD

● Line a baking sheet with parchment paper.

● Boil the maple syrup and corn syrup over medium heat in a 2-quart saucepan to 236°F, stirring occasionally with a heatproof spatula. Remove the syrup from the heat, and stir in the peanut butter and salt until they are incorporated. Stir in the peanuts and oats. Quickly drop by spoonfuls onto the parchment paper. If desired, sprinkle flakey sea salt on top. Let cool at room temperature. Store on layers of parchment paper in an airtight container. The pralines will be sticky on the first day, and then they'll crystallize overnight.

Baking sheet

Parchment paper

2-quart saucepan

Candy thermometer

Heatproof silicone spatula

Large spoon

1¼ cups maple syrup

¼ cup corn syrup

½ cup peanut butter

1 teaspoon kosher salt

1 cup peanuts, roasted

1¼ cups oats

Flakey sea salt, for sprinkling (optional)

Vanilla Marshmallows

MAKES 96 marshmallows

Perfect with rich hot cocoa or enjoyed simply on their own, homemade marshmallows are tastier, fluffier, and fresher than anything you can buy.

METHOD

● Spray a 10 x 15-inch jellyroll pan liberally with oil.

● Pour ¾ cup cold water into the bowl of a stand mixer, and sprinkle the gelatin on top. Stir with a fork until the gelatin is moistened and free of lumps.

● Bring 1 cup water, sugar, cream of tartar, and salt to a boil in a 3-quart saucepan over medium-high heat, stirring occasionally with a heatproof spatula until the sugar dissolves. If necessary, wash down the sides of the pan with a wet pastry brush to dissolve any sugar granules. Boil to 250°F. Remove from the heat, and let cool to 212°F, about 15 minutes.

● Meanwhile, use a heatproof spatula to break the bloomed gelatin in the mixer bowl into small pieces. When the syrup has cooled to 212°F, pour it over the gelatin, and stir until the gelatin is melted. Whip with the whisk attachment in the stand mixer for 1 minute on low speed. Increase speed to high, and whip for about 5 minutes, until very fluffy and thick. Add the vanilla extract down the side of the bowl, and whip for 30 seconds more. Pour the mixture into the prepared jellyroll pan, and spread evenly with an offset spatula. Let set overnight.

● Mix the cornstarch and powdered sugar in a large bowl. Remove the marshmallow slab from the pan and place it on a cutting board. Use a chef's knife and a ruler or straightedge to cut the marshmallows into 1¼-inch squares, tossing with the cornstarch mixture to prevent sticking. Shake the marshmallows in a sieve to remove any excess cornstarch, and store in an airtight container.

10 x 15-inch jellyroll pan

5-quart stand mixer with whisk attachment

Fork

3-quart saucepan

Heatproof silicone spatula

Pastry brush

Candy thermometer

Offset spatula

Large bowl

Cutting board

Chef's knife

Ruler or straightedge

Sieve

Oil for the pan

¾ cup cold water

3 tablespoons (3 envelopes) unflavored gelatin

1 cup water

3¼ cups sugar

½ teaspoon cream of tartar

⅛ teaspoon kosher salt

¾ teaspoon vanilla extract (page 130)

1 cup cornstarch

½ cup powdered sugar

Strawberry Lemonade Marshmallows

MAKES *192 marshmallows*

This pretty two-layer marshmallow will surprise you with its uncanny resemblance to a favorite summer beverage.

METHOD

● Spray two 10 x 15-inch jellyroll pans liberally with oil.

● For the lemon marshmallow layer, pour ¼ cup cold water and the lemon juice into the bowl of the stand mixer, and sprinkle the gelatin on top. Stir with a fork until the gelatin is moistened and free of lumps.

● Bring 1 cup water, sugar, cream of tartar, and salt to a boil in a 3-quart saucepan over medium-high heat, stirring occasionally with a heatproof spatula until the sugar dissolves. If necessary, wash down the sides of the pan with a wet pastry brush to dissolve any sugar granules. Boil to 250°F. Remove from the heat, and let cool to 212°F, about 15 minutes.

● Meanwhile, use the heatproof spatula to break the bloomed gelatin in the mixer bowl into small pieces. When the syrup has cooled to 212°F, pour it over the gelatin, and stir until the gelatin is melted.

● Whip the mixture with the whisk attachment in the stand mixer for 1 minute on low speed. Increase speed to high, and whip for about 5 minutes, until the mixture is very fluffy and beginning to hold its shape. Add the lemon zest, and whip for 30 seconds more. Pour half of the mixture into each prepared pan, and, working quickly, spread each evenly with an offset spatula. Then make the strawberry marshmallow layer.

● For the strawberry marshmallow layer, place the puréed strawberries in the bowl of the stand mixer, sprinkle the gelatin on top of the strawberries, and stir with a fork until the gelatin is moistened and free of lumps.

● Bring 1 cup water, sugar, cream of tartar, and salt to a boil in a 3-quart saucepan over medium-high heat, stirring occasionally with a heatproof spatula until the sugar dissolves. If necessary, wash down the sides of the pan with a wet pastry brush to dissolve any sugar granules. Boil to 250°F. Remove from the heat, and let cool to 212°F, about 15 minutes.

(continued)

YOU WILL NEED

Two 10 x 15-inch jellyroll pans

5-quart stand mixer with whisk attachment

Fork

3-quart saucepan

Heatproof silicone spatula

Pastry brush

Candy thermometer

Offset spatula

Large bowl

Cutting board

Chef's knife

Ruler or straightedge

Sieve

FOR THE LEMON MARSHMALLOW LAYER:

Oil for the pans

¼ cup cold water

½ cup lemon juice, from 4 to 5 lemons

3 tablespoons (3 envelopes) unflavored gelatin

1 cup water

3¼ cups sugar

½ teaspoon cream of tartar

⅛ teaspoon kosher salt

1 teaspoon lemon zest, finely grated

FOR THE STRAWBERRY MARSHMALLOW LAYER:

¾ cup puréed strawberries (about 12 ounces strawberries)

3 tablespoons (3 envelopes) unflavored gelatin

1 cup water

3¼ cups sugar

½ teaspoon cream of tartar

⅛ teaspoon kosher salt

2 cups cornstarch

1 cup powdered sugar

● Meanwhile, use a heatproof spatula to break the bloomed gelatin in the mixer bowl into small pieces. When the syrup has cooled to 212°F, pour it over the gelatin, and stir until the gelatin is melted.

● Place the bowl in the mixer, and whip with the whisk attachment for 1 minute on low speed. Increase the speed to high, and whip for about 5 minutes, until the mixture is very fluffy and beginning to hold its shape. Pour half of the strawberry mixture into each prepared pan on top of the lemon marshmallow layer, and, working quickly, spread each evenly with an offset spatula. Let set overnight.

● Mix the cornstarch and powdered sugar in a large bowl. Remove the marshmallow slabs from the pans and place them on a cutting board. Use the chef's knife and the ruler or straightedge to cut the marshmallows into 1¼-inch squares, tossing with the cornstarch mixture to prevent sticking. Shake the marshmallows in the sieve to remove any excess cornstarch, and store in an airtight container.

Chocolate Stars

MAKES *36 stars*

This technique can be used for chocolate molds of any shape and with any type of chocolate, but only white chocolate can be colored to impressive effect. The addition of luster dust, an edible powder that sparkles when it dries, adds shimmery appeal to these treats.

→

YOU WILL NEED

Narrow paintbrush (if using optional luster dust)

3 star-shaped chocolate molds with 12 cavities each

Large spoon

Offset spatula

Parchment paper

Edible luster dust (optional)

Dry powder food coloring such as red, white, blue, or yellow (optional)

12 ounces white chocolate, tempered (page 20), or melting chocolate

METHOD

● Use a narrow paintbrush to apply the luster dust, if using, to each cavity of the molds.

● Mix food coloring, if using, into the tempered white chocolate. Use a large spoon to fill each cavity to the top with chocolate. Tap the molds on the counter to release any air bubbles. Remove any excess chocolate by scraping the top of the molds with an offset spatula. Refrigerate until set, about 20 minutes. Unmold by flipping the molds upside down on a piece of parchment paper, and tapping on the edge of the mold with the handle of an offset spatula. Store in an airtight container.

Coconut Shells

MAKES *40 shells*

With a creamy marshmallow filling and a glossy chocolate shell, these show-stopping confections look and taste like coconuts. If you don't have enough molds to make the full recipe, have an oiled pan ready to pour the extra marshmallow into for free-form snacking.

METHOD

● With a narrow silicone brush, paint three tempered dark chocolate dots in each mold. These will be the "eyes" of the coconut. With a wide silicone brush, paint a ⅛-inch-thick layer of tempered milk chocolate in each mold. Scrape off any uneven tops with an offset spatula. This step can be done in advance.

● In the bowl of a stand mixer, sprinkle the gelatin on top of ¾ cup cold water, and stir with a fork until the gelatin is moistened and free of lumps.

● Bring 1 cup water, sugar, cream of tartar, and salt to a boil in a 3-quart saucepan over medium-high heat, stirring occasionally with a heatproof spatula until the sugar dissolves. If sugar crystals cling to the sides of the pan, dissolve them away with a wet pastry brush. Boil to 250°F. Remove the syrup from the heat, and let cool to 212°F, about 15 minutes.

● Meanwhile, use the heatproof spatula to cut the bloomed gelatin in the mixer bowl into small pieces. When the syrup has cooled to 212°F, pour it over the gelatin, and stir until the gelatin is melted. Place the bowl in the mixer, and whip with the whisk attachment for 1 minute on low speed. Increase the speed to high, and whip for about 5 minutes, until the mixture is very fluffy and begins to hold its shape. Stop the mixer, and add the vanilla extract, coconut, and macadamia nuts. Whip on low until incorporated, about 30 seconds.

● Working quickly, fill a piping bag with the marshmallow mixture. Pipe into the molds, which have already been coated with chocolate, leaving the top ⅛ inch of the cavity empty. Let set overnight.

● Use a ladle to pour the tempered milk chocolate into one mold at a time, over the set marshmallow fillings. Spread with a large offset spatula to completely cover the backs of the marshmallows. Let set. Flip the molds over onto parchment paper, and tap the edges with the handle of an offset spatula to release the coconut shells. Store in an airtight container.

Tip: *If you don't have any molds, these coconut marshmallows are delicious plain or dipped in chocolate according to the instructions on page 27.*

YOU WILL NEED

5 chocolate molds with eight 2¼-inch-wide demi-sphere cavities

Narrow silicone brush

Wide silicone brush

Offset spatula

5-quart stand mixer with whisk attachment

Fork

3-quart saucepan

Heatproof silicone spatula

Pastry brush

Candy thermometer

Piping bag

Ladle

Parchment paper

4 ounces dark chocolate, tempered (page 20) or melting chocolate

2 pounds milk chocolate, tempered (page 20) or coating chocolate, melted

3 tablespoons (3 envelopes) unflavored gelatin

¾ cup cold water

1 cup water

3¼ cups sugar

½ teaspoon cream of tartar

⅛ teaspoon kosher salt

¼ teaspoon vanilla extract (page 130)

2 cups finely shredded dried coconut

½ cup roasted macadamia nuts, finely chopped (optional)

1 pound milk chocolate, tempered (page 20)

Pastel Butter Mints

MAKES ABOUT 1¹/₄ pound

Soft and melt-in-your-mouth creamy, these mints are perfectly refreshing.

Baking sheet

Parchment paper

5-quart stand mixer

Food-safe gloves

Chef's knife

METHOD

● Line a baking sheet with parchment paper.

● Place the powdered sugar, cream, butter, and mint extract in the bowl of a stand mixer. Beat on low with a paddle attachment until thoroughly combined. Increase the speed to medium, and beat until the mixture clumps around the paddle.

● Divide the resulting "dough" into batches, one batch for each color of mint you're making. Apply drops of food coloring to each batch, aiming for pastel colors. Knead one batch with gloved hands, until the color is uniform. Wash the gloves, and repeat for each batch.

● Roll the dough into ½-inch-wide ropes, and then cut each rope into ½-inch-long pieces. Arrange the pieces on the prepared baking sheet so they don't touch each other. Let sit out uncovered overnight to dry. Store in an airtight container.

Tip: *Dividing the dough before you add the coloring allows you to make multiple colors from one batch. Without food coloring, the mints will be a light cream color.*

4¾ cups powdered sugar

2 tablespoons cream

½ cup butter, softened

1 teaspoon mint extract

Food coloring as desired, 6 to 8 drops

Candy Essentials
In the Pantry

We've talked about the luscious, silken, delicately crunchy, and all around incredible qualities of chocolate and sugar—they manifest beautiful creations and are the kings and queens of the candy world. But what about the unsung heroes of candymaking? Peanut Brittle wouldn't be its delightful self without the peanuts. And billowy, cloud-like Vanilla Marshmallows simply wouldn't *be* if it weren't for vanilla extract. The following recipes will help you stock your pantry with flavors and garnishes essential to candymaking, and they may just infuse your imagination with taste inventions of your own!

Vanilla Extract

MAKES 1 quart

It's very easy to make vanilla extract at home—and it's so good!
Try using a combination of different kinds of vanilla for a flavor that's
uniquely your own. Decanted into a decorative bottle, this homemade
vanilla makes a very special gift.

YOU WILL NEED

1-quart glass jar with lid

METHOD

● In a 1-quart glass jar, mix together the brandy, vodka, vanilla pods and
seeds, and vanilla extract, if using. Place the lid on the jar, and let the
mixture sit in a cool, dark place. It needs to sit for 3 months; add used
vanilla beans from baking, as available. Decant 4 ounces of the vanilla
extract into a small, decorative bottle, and top up the jar with fresh
brandy or vodka—the extract will last indefinitely this way.

Tip: *The optional vanilla extract in this recipe helps boost the flavor
quickly, but it's not required.*

1²/₃ cup brandy

1²/₃ cup vodka

5 vanilla beans, Tahitian
or Bourbon, split and
seeds scraped

3 ounces vanilla extract,
Tahitian or Bourbon
(optional)

Vanilla extract adds
a sweet flavor to these
meringues (page 54).

Candied Citrus Peel

MAKES ABOUT 9 ounces

This ingredient is deliciously versatile. A treat on its own or dipped in chocolate, candied citrus peel can also serve as an accent on top of or mixed into another type of candy, such as nougat or caramel.

→ YOU WILL NEED

Paring knife

3-quart saucepan

Sieve

3   oranges, 5 lemons,
    or 2 grapefruits

2   cups water

2   cups sugar

¼   cup corn syrup or
    ¼ teaspoon cream
    of tartar

Pinch kosher salt

● With a paring knife, cut a thin slice off the tops and bottoms of each piece of fruit. Score the peel in 1-inch-wide strips, cutting just through the pith. Use your fingers to carefully peel off the strips of citrus peel.

● Place the peels in a 3-quart saucepan, and add water to cover. Bring to a boil over medium-high heat, and then reduce the heat so the mixture gently simmers. Let cook 20 minutes, until tender. Drain the peels in a sieve.

● If the peels and piths are thicker than ¼ inch, use a paring knife or spoon to scrape away the pith until the strips are ¼ inch thick. Cut the peels lengthwise into ¼-inch strips.

● In the saucepan, combine the water, sugar, corn syrup or cream of tartar, and salt. Bring to a boil over medium-high heat. Add the trimmed citrus peel, and reduce the heat to low, so the mixture gently simmers. Cook until the peel is completely translucent and tender, about 30 to 45 minutes. Remove from the heat, and pour the peels and syrup into a heatproof container. Let sit overnight at room temperature, and then store the peel in its cooking syrup in the refrigerator.

● To cover the peel in sugar, remove the peel from syrup, and let it dry out overnight before rolling in granulated sugar.

Roasted Nuts

MAKES 1 pound

Applying a "low and slow" cooking method to nuts enhances their flavor compared to toasting them at a high temperature for a short time. They also cook more evenly and are less likely to scorch. You can roast any amount of nuts at a time, but they will last for a while so larger batches are a good idea.

Baking sheet

Parchment paper or silicone mat

1 pound nuts, such as almonds, pecans, walnuts, pistachios

METHOD

● Preheat the oven to 250°F.

● Line a baking sheet with parchment paper or a silicone mat. Spread out the nuts on the baking sheet so that they are in a single layer. If roasting more than one kind of nut, keep them separate, and check each for doneness separately since they cook at different rates. Walnuts, for example, will be done in about 30 minutes while almonds will take about 60 minutes. Roast until they are evenly browned inside, stirring every 20 minutes.

Candied Ginger

MAKES ABOUT 1 pound

For the most tender and flavorful results, be sure to use young, juicy, and non-fibrous pieces of fresh ginger.

→

METHOD

● Place a cooling rack on a piece of parchment paper.

● Peel the ginger with a vegetable peeler or the edge of a spoon, and cut it into coin-shaped slices, ⅛-inch thick. Boil ginger and 4 cups water, covered, over medium-high heat in a 3-quart saucepan until the ginger is tender, about 40 minutes. Measure out ¼ cup of the ginger liquid and reserve. Drain the ginger, and then return it to the pot.

● Add the sugar and the reserved ginger liquid, and bring it to a boil over medium-high heat. Reduce the heat to medium, and stir the syrup frequently with a heatproof spatula until it boils away and the sugar begins to re-crystallize. Immediately remove the saucepan from the heat, and transfer the ginger to the cooling rack. Spread the ginger out with the spatula, and separate into individual pieces. Let cool, and store in an airtight container.

YOU WILL NEED

Cooling rack

Parchment paper

Vegetable peeler or spoon

Chef's knife

3-quart saucepan

Strainer

Heatproof spatula

1 pound fresh ginger

4 cups water

2½ cups sugar

Acknowledgments

First and foremost, I'd like to thank my family, especially my mom and dad, who taught me that the only thing better than eating good food is to share it. I'd also like to thank Carolyn Wong, owner of Carolyn Wong Cakes, whose taste buds and suggestions were invaluable in the creation of this collection of recipes.

I'd like to thank everyone at Lark, especially Beth Sweet and Kristi Pfeffer, for their editorial and creative support of all things candy. Deep gratitude is offered to the amazing White on Rice Couple, Todd Porter and Diane Cu, for capturing these gorgeous photos. Many thanks to Kathy Sheldon, for lending her copyediting finesse to these pages, and appreciation goes to Eileen Paulin and Erika Kotite.

Warm thanks to all of those who have influenced, helped, taught, and generally enlivened me during my candymaking adventures. Both this cookbook and my company, BonBonBar Confections, have benefited from so much kind encouragement and generosity. Thanks to: Annie Baker, Matt Bercovitz, Chad Boyda, Michael Boyda, CJ Calvert, The Candy Store (Diane, Brian, and Liana), Jun Chen, Tania Clucas, Stephen Durfee, Evelyn FitzGibbon, Foodzie, Clemence Gossett, Joyce Guan, Clarine Lim Hardesty, Marie and Darrell Jackson, Jodi Koenig, Dafna Kory, Susannah Lescher, Pouneh Rajaii, Marika Shimamoto-Doob, Chuck Siegel, Jeri Sisco, Anastasia Widiarsih, and Bonnie Yu.

About the Author

Nina Wanat was born in Brooklyn, New York, and raised in New Jersey. She initially moved to California for the film industry, but she stayed for the food. After dropping out of law school, she studied baking and pastry at the Culinary Institute of America at Greystone and apprenticed with artisan chocolatiers. In 2007, she founded BonBonBar Confections, which specializes in handmade candy bars, caramels, and marshmallows. She lives in San Francisco.

METRIC CONVERSION CHART BY VOLUME
(for Liquids)

U.S.	Metric (milliliters/liters)
¼ teaspoon	1.25 mL
½ teaspoon	2.5 mL
1 teaspoon	5 mL
1 tablespoon	15 mL
¼ cup	60 mL
½ cup	120 mL
¾ cup	180 mL
1 cup	240 mL
2 cups (1 pint)	480 mL
4 cups (1 quart)	960 mL
4 quarts (1 gallon)	3.8 L

METRIC CONVERSION CHART BY WEIGHT
(for Dry Ingredients)

U.S.	Metric (grams/kilograms)
¼ teaspoon	1 g
½ teaspoon	2 g
1 teaspoon	5 g
1 tablespoon	15 g
16 ounces (1 pound)	450 g
2 pounds	900 g
3 pounds	1.4 kg
4 pounds	1.8 kg
5 pounds	2.3 kg
6 pounds	2.7 kg

COOKING MEASUREMENT EQUIVALENTS

3 teaspoons = 1 tablespoon

2 tablespoons = 1 fluid ounce

4 tablespoons = ¼ cup

5 tablespoons + 1 teaspoon = ⅓ cup

8 tablespoons = ½ cup

10 tablespoons + 2 teaspoons = ⅔ cup

12 tablespoons = ¾ cup

16 tablespoons = 1 cup

48 teaspoons = 1 cup

1 cup = 8 fluid ounces

2 cups = 1 pint

2 pints = 1 quart

4 quarts = 1 gallon

TEMPERATURE CONVERSION

Fahrenheit	Celsius
32°	0°
212°	100°
250°	121°
275°	135°
300°	149°
350°	177°
375°	191°
400°	204°
425°	218°

METRIC CONVERSIONS

Index